Collective Student Efficacy

Collective Student Efficacy

Developing Independent and Inter-Dependent Learners

John Hattie

Douglas Fisher

Nancy Frey

Shirley Clarke

FOR INFORMATION:

Corwin
A SAGE Company
2455 Teller Road
Thousand Oaks, California 91320
(800) 233-9936
www.corwin.com

SAGE Publications Ltd.
1 Oliver's Yard
55 City Road
London EC1Y 1SP
United Kingdom

SAGE Publications India Pvt. Ltd.
B 1/I 1 Mohan Cooperative Industrial Area
Mathura Road, New Delhi 110 044
India

SAGE Publications Asia-Pacific Pte. Ltd.
18 Cross Street #10-10/11/12
China Square Central
Singapore 048423

President: Mike Soules
Associate Vice President
  and Editorial Director: Monica Eckman
Executive Editor: Tori Mello Bachman
Associate Editor: Eliza B. Erickson
Project Editor: Amy Schroller
Copy Editor: Lynne Curry
Typesetter: C&M Digitals (P) Ltd.
Proofreader: Susan Schon
Indexer: Integra
Cover Designer: Scott Van Atta
Marketing Manager: Deena Meyer

Printed in Canada

ISBN 978-1-5443-8344-6

This book is printed on acid-free paper.

21 22 23 24 25 10 9 8 7 6 5 4 3 2 1

Contents

Acknowledgments

Writing a book with three colleagues, living in the UK, USA, and Oz, from different perspectives, bringing together many different aspects of our work and the scattered research on the topic—has been a case study of collective efficacy. We know each other and have worked together before so the trust, joy, and confidence in working as a team was high; the ability to contribute to the group discussions was never a problem; and we built the confidence to believe that the collective work would be better than if any one of us worked alone. There were many debates—some hard fought; there were many times we needed to go back to the research and into the schools to anchor our arguments; and the flow and overall tone we were aiming at took many iterations. Most of all, there is an enjoyment and feeling of pride at completing this book as it opens a new topic, or at least provides a new lens bringing together many well-known ideas.

We would like to thank the following educators, for their exciting contributions to this book: The many teachers involved in Shirley's "learning teams" over the last few years, experimenting and evaluating formative assessment strategies; and in particular Becky Carlzon, Bangkok Patina International School, Bangkok; Emma Shiland, Ysgol Glan Gele Infant School, Abergele, Wales; Aaron Hall, Thomas Bullock Primary School, Norwich, England; and the teachers and students at Health Sciences High & Middle College, San Diego, California.

Publisher's Acknowledgments

Corwin gratefully acknowledges the contributions of the following reviewers:

Melody (Dani) Aldrich
Reading Specialist, Casa Grande High School

About the Authors

John Hattie, PhD, is an award-winning education researcher and best-selling author with nearly thirty years of experience examining what works best in student learning and achievement. His research, better known as Visible Learning®, is a culmination of nearly thirty years synthesizing more than 1,500 meta-analyses comprising more than ninety thousand studies involving over 300 million students around the world. He has presented and keynoted in over 350 international conferences and has received numerous recognitions for his contributions to education. His notable publications include *Visible Learning*, *Visible Learning for Teachers*, *Visible Learning and the Science of How We Learn*, *Visible Learning for Mathematics, Grades K–12*, and, most recently, *10 Mindframes for Visible Learning: Teaching for Success*.

Douglas Fisher, PhD, is professor and chair of educational leadership at San Diego State University and a leader at Health Sciences High and Middle College having been an early intervention teacher and elementary school educator. He is the recipient of an International Reading Association William S. Gray Citation of Merit, a Kent Williamson Exemplary Leader Award from the Conference on English Leadership of NCTE, as well as a Christa McAuliffe Award for Excellence in Teacher Education. He has published numerous articles on reading and literacy, differentiated instruction, and curriculum design as well as books, such as *PLC+: Better Decisions and Greater Impact by Design, Building Equity: Policies and Practices to Empower All Learners*, and *Developing Assessment-Capable Visible Learners, Grades K-12*. He can be reached at dfisher@mail.sdsu.edu.

Nancy Frey, PhD, is a professor in educational leadership at San Diego State University and a leader at Health Sciences High and Middle College. She has been a special education teacher, reading specialist, and administrator in public schools. Nancy has engaged in Professional Learning Communities as a member and in designing schoolwide systems to improve teaching and learning for all students. She has published numerous books, including *The Teacher Clarity Playbook, Grades K-12*, and *Rigorous Reading*.

Shirley Clarke, MEd, Honorary Doctorate, is a world expert in formative assessment, specializing in the practical application of its principles. Many thousands of teachers have worked with Shirley or read her books and, through them, the practice of formative assessment is continually evolving, developing and helping to transform students' achievements.

Shirley's latest publications are *Unlocking Learning Intentions and Success Criteria, Formative Assessment, Visible Learning Feedback* with John Hattie, and *Thinking Classrooms* with Katherine Muncaster. Her website www.shirleyclarke-education.org contains a video streaming platform of clips of formative assessment in action as well as detailed feedback from her action research teams.

INTRODUCTION

WHY COLLECTIVE EFFICACY?

In theory, there is wisdom in the crowd. As we will see, that is only true sometimes, under some conditions. But when it works, the collective is very powerful and can actually accelerate learning. Before we turn our attention to the ways in which teachers can mobilize collective efficacy in their classrooms, let's explore the idea of the collective a bit further.

David Deming (2017) noted that employment for low-skilled production and trade jobs shrank in the 1980s. In the 1990s, a "hollowing out" of the labor market occurred as computers both substituted for labor in routine tasks requiring mid-level skills and complemented high-skilled labor. Further, since computers have begun to automate "cognitive" tasks, the employment rate in high-paying jobs has shown little or no growth since 2000. But tasks that required social skills started to increase, primarily, he argues, because computers are still very poor substitutes for tasks where programmers don't know "the rules" and where the skills of social sensitivity are critical. In these social aspects, computers have yet to pass what is known as the Turing test. In 1950, Alan Turing proposed the following test: An interviewer asks written questions of two respondents and is given the task of determining which respondent is human and which is a computer. Turing proposed that a machine would pass the test once it could convince a human 70 percent of the time after five minutes of conversation.

Deming traced the employment rates in the United States from 1980 onward for those with science skills (especially math and science, but our hunch is that this would apply to many other domains). He divided

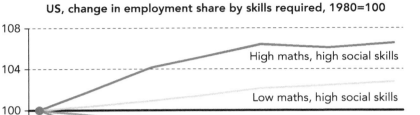

US, change in employment share by skills required, 1980=100

High maths, high social skills

Low maths, high social skills

High maths, low social skills

Low maths, low social skills

1980   90   2000   06   12

Source: "The Growing Importance of Social Skills in the Labor Market", by David Deming, Aug. 2016.

Figure 0.1

individuals with the math (or science) skills into two groups—those above and below the median. (He called them "high" and "low," although a clearer picture is seen if we call them "higher" or "lower"—as low can, in this case, falsely mean negligible skills). Figure 0.1 shows that occupations with higher math and higher social skill requirements have grown robustly throughout the wage distribution, and jobs with higher social skill and lower math requirements have also grown, although they are mostly concentrated in the bottom two-thirds of the wage distribution. Jobs with high social skill requirements have experienced greater relative growth, but employment and wage growth has been strongest in jobs that require high levels of *both* cognitive and social skills.

Deming's conclusion is that nearly all job growth since 1980 has been in occupations that demand social skills working in collectives. Jobs that require high levels of analytical and mathematical reasoning but low levels of social interaction have fared poorly. We see his work as showing the critical importance of developing collective student efficacy— alongside and indeed implicit to also developing precious knowledge. Employers want team players, translators, communicators, and those with high social sensitivity along with the previously valued knowledge.

We suspect that employers find it difficult to teach seventeen to twenty-year-olds these social skills but find it relatively easier to educate them in the content skills of the specific vocation. Thus, if we do not teach students the skills of collective efficacy, then we may be helping make them unemployable. Hence, the imperative of this book.

In the chapters that follow, we explore the components of collective student efficacy that can, and should, be taught. We start Chapter 1 visiting a classroom where the students are accustomed to working together in ways that build their collective efficacy, and we identify the vital components and success criteria for students' collective efficacy. In Chapter 2, we visit the evidence base that informs our ideas and rec-· ommendations. It may surprise you, given what you know about us as authors, to learn that there is no meta-analysis or even a set of studies that could be used to create a meta-analysis on collective student efficacy. However, there is a significant amount of evidence that can be used to inform decisions about building collective student efficacy.

Chapters 3 and 4 explore the critical "I" and "We" skills that are going to be important in the development and successful enactment of lessons involving collective efficacy. Learning to work in a collective is not a given for many students, as they may have limited awareness of themselves and how they interact with others, and limited awareness of group norms, sharing, and giving, and learning from others. We identify a set of specific "I" and "We" skills that need to be developed to ensure students have the skills and the confidence to contribute and confidence in the group processes and probability of success.

In Chapter 5, we explore the nature of learning design and preparing lessons for ensuring students have opportunities to engage in collective efficacy. If we consider that developing collective efficacy skills is important in our lessons, it is necessary that there is constructive alignment between the learning intentions, the tasks, and the success criteria. These issues are explored in Chapter 6. There are also important structures we can use to maximize the value of these skills, such as student roles in the collective, optimal group size, and awareness of the possible barriers to success (Chapter 7). Complementing the intent of the lessons and the structures to enable collective efficacy there must be constructive alignment with the assessments. If the final assessments are more focused on the individual, then this can have marked negative effects on the value and development of collective skills, but major issues also arise if only group assessment occurs. These issues are covered in Chapter 8. We conclude in Chapter 9 by revisiting the major themes.

CHAPTER 1

THE VALUE OF
THE COLLECTIVE

"Welcome to history! Today is an exciting day because we are using all of the information you gathered this past week to demonstrate our understanding of the significance of Greek mythology on the lives of everyday people of the time. AND we get to discuss the ways in which Greek mythology survives to this day. But that's a little advance warning about next week when we bring all of this learning forward to modern times. Are you all ready? Any clarifying questions before we begin?"

Brianna Fernandez's sixth grade students have been learning about the geographic, political, economic, religious, and social structures of the early civilizations of Ancient Greece for several weeks. Her class is organized into partners and teams. Some tasks are assigned to individual students, others to pairs, and still others to teams. As she notes, "When it's team time, I combine partners so that students who have been working together are still together, but just in a larger grouping. I find that the teams push each other's thinking and they are more likely to use their argumentation skills when the groups are a little bigger. And I think that our whole class discussions are richer because of these various groupings."

Intentionally assigning tasks to individuals, or groups, (see more on pp. 83–86).

Before she can go on, Cassie raises her hand and asks, "I know that Zeus had a lot of kids, but who is the mother?" Ms. Fernandez responds, "That's a great question. We haven't really talked about that. And there are a lot of stories for us to learn. Can we add that to our investigations wall?" Smiling, Cassie says, "Yes, please. Maybe my group can take on that investigation when we finish today."

> ### Learning From a Distance
>
> If teaching from a distance, the investigations wall might be a shared Google doc. Once groups select an investigation, they can collaborate. Most platforms allow for students to interact with one another in some type of a breakout room, which can be organized in pairs or larger groups. The learning expectations do not need to change for this lesson to be effective from a distance.

Questioning, (see more on pp. 61–64).

The students in Ms. Fernandez's class are used to asking questions as part of their learning. Ms. Fernandez knows that her students must learn the content and she knows that there is a thrill that comes when students are able to go deeper and explore aspects of the curriculum that interest them. In fact, her students keep learning about history outside of their time in her class because of the investigations wall questions. These questions are posed by individuals and groups. Then, groups of students can select from the questions for their collaborative investigations. Ms. Fernandez provides time for groups to share what they have learned relative to their investigations at the end of each class period.

"Any other questions before we begin?" asks Ms. Fernandez. Hearing none, she moves into the learning for the day. She says, "Now that we know a lot about the many gods from ancient Greece, we want to understand how these gods impacted daily life. So, our learning intentions are on the board." She pointed out the following statements:

Learning intentions for individual and the group, (see more in Chapter 6).

- I am learning about the impact of Greek mythology on the lives of everyday people. (knowledge)
- We are learning how to be open to other ideas, opinions, and perspectives while we try to reach consensus. (working together)
- We are learning how to extract information from a range of sources. (transferable skill)

In Ms. Fernandez's class, there are whole class learning intentions, which are typically focused on the content knowledge or skills each student needs to learn. And there are learning intentions for collective learning, often focused on the role of working as a team. Of course, there are also times in which the class learning intentions are to develop a specific transferable skill, such as developing communication skills or specific writing applications, and there are times when the collective learning is centered on content, such as might be the case when students are engaged in a debate or using the Jigsaw method. More on individual and group learning intentions can be found in Chapter 6, and Jigsaw in Chapter 5.

A key skill the students need to use in their learning about Greece, gathering information from a range of resources, is one that they have visited before. On this occasion, Ms. Fernandez simply brings up the process success criteria for this skill and reminds them of the elements. When they first encountered this skill, some months ago, the teacher had co-constructed the success criteria with her students. She demonstrated how she found information on buildings in ancient Egypt that were influenced by the Egyptian burial customs. In the previous lesson, she demonstrated her thinking aloud while reading an informational source. During that previous lesson, she paused and asked the class "What did I just do?" Sometimes she deliberately does something which is not helpful, such as making her search too broad and getting annoyed or copying information word-for-word from the source and then running out of time. When she demonstrates these errors, she asks the class, "What should I have done differently?" When this happens, she invites students to quickly confer in their pairs and she selects a random pair to comment.

Learning From a Distance

Think alouds, like the one Ms. Fernandez used, can be recorded and provided for students in an asynchronous environment. Interactive videos are useful as students can engage with the content several times in preparation for their synchronous lessons or as review of previously learning. Embedding questions in the video, using a platform such as PlayPosit or Edpuzzle, allows teachers to check for understanding and take note of areas they should focus on in future lessons.

Thinking strategies in groups, (see more on p. 93).

Their previous learning, focused on Egypt, ended with the following success criterion:

We are learning to extract information from a range of sources.

In addition, they developed a number of reminders that they can use as a checklist of sorts to ensure that they were successful. The reminders included the following:

Teacher clarity, (see more on pp. 96–97).

- Make your search clear and focused (e.g., how antibiotics work)

- In a book, use the index carefully in case some things are grouped together

- Focus on key information (names, dates, main points)

- Write in notes, not whole sentences

- Keep different issues separated with titles, for easy access

Success criteria for individual and groups, (see more in Chapter 6).

Returning to the new lesson on Greek mythology and the impact of those beliefs on everyday life, Ms. Fernandez shared the success criteria for her students' *individual* learning of the knowledge:

- I can identify the impact of ancient Greek beliefs on women.

- I can explain why ancient Greeks built monuments, buildings, and statues to honor their gods.

- I can describe how ancient Greeks resolved conflicts.

Ms. Fernandez also shares success criteria for the *group* learning intention (We are learning how to be open to other ideas, opinions, and perspectives while we try to reach consensus). Given the major task for the class period, Ms. Fernandez reminds students to use their group norms checklist. Sometimes success has many options and some of the options may not be required. The checklist included the following:

- Ask questions and seek clarification from others.

- Participate actively in the discussion.

- Listen carefully without interrupting.

- Think about what is being said by others.

- Paraphrase what you think others have said to check your understanding and listening skills.

- Invite people to share ideas and opinions.

- Provide reasons for disagreement with others.

Learning questions, (see more on pp. 64–68.

Clarity in terms of learning intentions and success criteria helps students make sense of the lesson. As we have noted elsewhere, students should be able to answer three questions (Fisher et al., 2016):

- What am I learning today?

- Why am I learning it?

- How will I know that I learned it?

These questions apply to both individual and collective efforts. Students, just like all of the rest of us, are asking these questions irrespective of whether the tasks are individual or collaborative. Which brings us to the task Ms. Fernandez assigned. As she said, "Our first task today is a carousel. You'll see the large poster papers around the room, ready for you. Each of them has a specific topic. With your partner, please add information to the poster based on what you already know and have learned from the readings and videos. For round two, you'll ask clarifying questions of each other using sticky notes and then we'll divide up the questions and have some team investigations and presentations. This is just the start, to make sure that we all have the same general information about ancient Greek mythology."

Pairs and size of groups, (see more in Chapter 7).

Nature of the task: Additive, (see more in Chapter 7).

Learning From a Distance

Instead of a carousel in which students move around the room, Ms. Fernandez could use breakout rooms and rotate students through different tasks. She could use Google Slides to share the images. For example, in room one students may be viewing and discussing one image, taking notes in their digital notebooks. In the next room, they could see a different image and repeat the process, and so on until they have finish visiting all of the rooms.

At one poster, Leo and Brandi are talking about the definition of a citizen in ancient Greece. At another poster, Kayla and Sarai are talking about temples and other buildings. At a third poster, Abdul and Jay are talking about flaws that the various gods had. After two minutes, students rotate to another poster. The process continues for several rounds, then the task changes to focus on questions based on the information presented. After several question generation rounds, partners select questions to answer and start their work. For example, Leo and Brandi choose the question, "Why did they have so many festivals and celebrations for their gods?" Applying their key skill individual and group success criteria, students are encouraged to use the Internet and the various print resources around the room to respond to the questions that their peers generate.

Twenty-four minutes into the class period, Ms. Fernandez interrupts their work and invites them to participate in an online quiz that contains foundational information about Greek mythology. She does so to check their understanding and to determine if there are any gaps in their knowledge, the knowledge that they will need for the next task. Thus far, students have had opportunities to use and develop their individual knowledge

Formative feedback to the teacher, (see more on pp. 43–47, 76).

and to work collaboratively with a peer. In doing so, their individual learning was likely improved and they had a chance to reinforce their collaborative learning skills.

Learning From a Distance

Formative practice tests are a powerful way to engage students when they are provided opportunities to analyze their results. This can be done easily using a quiz tool (e.g., Quizlet or Kahoot!) that provides instant data for review. Based on their analyses, students can form study groups and engage in teaching one another. They can also select from a range of study skills to deepen their understanding.

Collective student efficacy: students' beliefs that by working with other people, they will learn more.

But they did not yet engage in collective efficacy. In the one study of individual and collective student efficacy, Pina-Neves, Faria, and Räty (2013) define the concept as "the beliefs the students share about their class being able to accomplish a certain academic task or activity as a group" (p. 455). Collective student efficacy (CSE) could also be described as students' confidence about their ability and disposition to successfully contribute to a task or accomplish an activity as part of a team. They also need to develop confidence that the group can lead to better outcomes for group members and the group, more than they could do by themselves. Our simplified, working definition of CSE (which is expanded later in this book) means the following: students' beliefs that by working with other people, they will learn more.

Building confidence to contribute to the group, (see more in Chapter 3).

Importantly, collective student efficacy takes time and is not simply a set of activities that happen in the class. The rest of this book focuses on the ways that teachers can facilitate collective efficacy with their students.

Three fundamental principles of SCE, (see more on p. 22).

But returning to Ms. Fernandez's classroom, students were reminded of the learning intentions for the day and then were introduced to the final task that would take them to the end of the class meeting. As Ms. Fernandez said, "For our next task, we'll be in our teams. There will be two teams for each success criteria. I have some questions for each success criteria that can guide your work, and of course, you probably have more questions. The goal is to really understand what is being explored in the success criteria. Your team can create a presentation or write an informational report, but remember that you'll be teaching members of other teams tomorrow and they will be teaching you. And then, next week, we'll have our debate and you'll need to know a lot of this for the debate. The debate will be about the most influential God and how that God impacted the people of Greece."

Learning From a Distance

When students have opportunities to set goals, make choices, seek feedback, and monitor their progress, they are much more likely to participate, engage, and see themselves as teachers. By providing these options in a distance learning setting, students can develop skills in decision-making and collaboration. This can be accomplished as students document their learning through video such as Flipgrid and seek feedback from others.

Leo, Brandi, Kayla, and Sarai are a team. As they begin their work, Brandi says, "Remember last time when Cassie's team tried to win the debate? She was asking really hard questions, but we knew it all. You guys really make me learn this stuff."

Sarai responded, "Like Ms. Fernandez says, learning isn't a competition, but I love the debates even when we don't agree with the side we're on. It's just fun to think about what the other side will say and then be ready for it."

Leo adds, "Yeah, our team is great. We help each other and make sure everyone is ready. I wish we could stay together the rest of the year. I always learn more when we get to work together."

Kayla reminds the group that they have work to do, adding, "So, do we want a presentation or a paper? I say paper because then we have more information ready for the debate. But what do you think?" The conversation continues:

Forms of assessment, (see more in Chapter 8).

Leo:	Yeah, a paper is probably a good idea, but can we have some main points like bullets so that I know the important things to tell the other groups?
Brandi:	Yeah, I agree. But this time can we make sure we have our sources, so we don't have to find them again next week? Just in case we can use any of them for the debate.

Kayla: Yep, good idea. So, that was easy. Now, about our topic, women in ancient Greece. I don't see how that is connected to the gods.

Sarai: Let's read the questions. [pause] Oh, interesting. There were female gods, but mortal women did not have many rights. Why would they make female gods and then not let women have rights?

Brandi: It says here that women couldn't vote and they usually did not get to pick who they got married to. It kinda sounds like Egypt.

Leo: So, their job was to be the mom? Could they do other work, too?

Kayla: But remember, women got the body ready for it to be buried. I think that's different than Egypt, but I might be wrong.

Leo: So, the women did have more purposes in Greece.

Sarai: Right, and religion gave them a purpose.

Kayla: But the society did not. They weren't even citizens.

Brandi: Yes, but they were really important because the gods made them take care of the dead and get them ready. Like that seems kinda powerful.

Leo: Right?

Kayla: But it would be more powerful to vote.

Sarai: And to pick your own husband.

Kayla: What are we going to write? Can you open a doc to share?

Leo: Yes, but was there anything from any of the gods that you studied that told women their role? Was it the gods or the people?

Brandi: Not the gods that I learned about. And nobody said anything about that during our roundtable.

Sarai: And there were female gods. So, I think that the problem is really the society.

The conversation continues and they jointly construct a text in which they outline the issues and respond to the questions and prompts provided by their teacher.

Learning from a Distance

There are a number of tools that allow students to jointly construct texts (e.g., Etherpad or Google Docs). Students can be in a video conference while writing and sharing ideas. In some cases, the students talk and one person at a time writes in a shared document. The idea is that the text contains contributions from all members of the group.

Much of their conversation focuses on the content at hand, but notice the beliefs that the members of this team have. They

- value the contributions of their peers,
- know that their opinions and ideas are worthy of consideration,
- display confidence in the team's collective ability,
- believe that their time together is useful,
- understand that they are each integral to the overall task completion,
- learn more as a result of their interactions, and
- use their individual (or as we call them "I") skills as well as collaborative (or as we call them "we") skills.

Developing collective mindframes, (see more on p. 67).

As we hope to show in the course of this book, collective student efficacy is more than cooperative and collaborative learning. Group tasks are important but do not necessarily result in the type of learning that we're talking about here. In addition to worthy tasks and clear expectations for learning, collective student efficacy requires the development and refinement of both individual and collective skills. In fact, we see them as building on each other over time. Students arrive to the group task with a set of knowledge, skills, and dispositions. They use those in service of completing a group task. When structured well, these group tasks build collective beliefs and simultaneously validate and extend those of the individual.

Think again about Sarai, Brandi, Leo, and Kayla. They arrived at this particular task with a set of skills, knowledge, and dispositions. Some of them knew more about women in ancient Greece (and Egypt) than others. Some had stronger reading and reasonings skills than others. Some had more motivation to learn the content than others. And some had stronger interpersonal, communication, and social skills than others.

Motivations for learning in a collective, (see more on p. 85).

Despite those differences, they came together to complete a task. And they believed that they could complete the task. In fact, they had evidence that they had successfully completed similar tasks in the past. As a result, they learned more. They believed that the experience was important, in part for tasks that could come in the future (the presentations and the debate). But even more importantly, they understood the value of the collective and the ways in which other people help us understand the world.

CHAPTER 2

WHY FOCUS ON COLLECTIVE STUDENT EFFICACY?

What do you remember from your days in school? Friends, great teachers, special events likely come to mind. But it is also likely you will recall the emphasis on collaborative learning, the plea that we need to develop team players, and the claim that there is no "I" in team (but there is "me"). We also recall an emphasis on personalized learning, on developing every child, and the equity claims about each and every child. At the same time, we have a model of schooling involving twenty to forty children in one room, grouped by age. We teachers are expected to deliver a curriculum often packaged with slabs of information and inquiry. We endlessly group students within classes aiming primarily for positive interactions and teamwork, but then we ask students to complete examinations and assignments by themselves and mark them individually. What a mixed set of messages.

Then as adults in schools, we are all subjected to seemingly endless meetings, sitting, usually listening, and so often think "I could use this time better," or when asked to work with others, reflect, "I could do it faster by myself." Then along comes the research, which notes that the new number one in Visible Learning® is "teachers' collective efficacy!" Hey, what?

Collective implies teams, the wisdom of the crowd, and learning from others; but most of us know that collaborative work is only worthwhile sometimes in some circumstances. Surely, not another set of edicts that teachers must meet more often to discuss their efficacy. Indeed, the very title, "collective efficacy" implies some kind of positive group think and invites a collective possibly without a purpose. The title would be more accurate if it were "teachers' collective efficacy *about their impact*," as it is not pertaining to confidence in the lesson plans, in the ways we teach, or in the structures and scheduling of classes. It is about understanding what high expectations mean, what at least a year's growth for a year's input means, what challenge in the curriculum means, and agreeing on what is sufficient evidence that a student has mastered the material enough to move to the next level. The core notion is agreeing on moderation of standards and doing this in a high trust, collective, and evidence-based manner. So, there must be a purpose to the concept of "collective efficacy."

There are oodles of resources available for groups to become a *collective*. Browse any airport bookstore and you'll see plenty of books about the wisdom of the crowd, how to get teams operating successfully, and the importance of leading the "collective" of people within companies, schools, and governments. The essence of leadership very much relates to managing people and groups, and in recent years a surge of interest has emerged in how leaders can create positive environments and high trust so that they can enact "collective efficacy" in order to optimize the success.

One of our observations from this vast literature on collective efficacy is that it is not easy: Not much evidence exists for the idea that every collective endeavor yields value, and there is little research support for the wisdom of the crowd. Collective efficacy has become a slogan, a mantra, and is applied to many situations that do not demand much of a collective, do not enable any collective to be enacted, or are not set up to succeed. Thus, despite the seductive appeal of the wisdom of the crowd or collective efficacy, there is little evidence to support these notions in many situations (Rowe, 2019). This is because many assume such wisdom is simply a function of putting individuals together and letting the cream rise. But each individual brings to the crowd a set of skills, specific expectations, and related beliefs about their role, the role of others, and the worthwhileness of working in a crowd. As we can all attest from our prior experience, working in groups has not been so profitable. It is easier to do a task by oneself and it can be too hard to manage the feelings, dominance, reticence, or distraction in a group.

But then, there is the evidence about collective efficacy and the impact it has on outcomes for groups. Perhaps some of the wisdom-of-the-crowd claims are missing key ingredients that make teams effective. Or perhaps there are some tasks that are simply not worth the collective effort. Let's explore the idea of the collective and consider ways in which teams can have greater impact on themselves and the outcomes of their efforts.

Collective Efficacy

Albert Bandura (Bandura & Walters, 1977) invented the term "collective efficacy" based on his observation that a group's confidence in its abilities seemed to be associated with greater success. In other words, the assurance or confidence a person places in his or her team affects the team's overall performance. This is core to the notion—it is not only confidence in the outcome of the team's work but confidence that working in a team can enhance outcomes. When a group of individuals share the belief that, through their unified efforts, they can overcome challenges and produce intended results, they *are* more effective. For example, in communities where neighbors share the belief that they can band together to overcome crime, violence is significantly less (Sampson, et al., 1997). In companies, when team members hold positive beliefs about the team's capabilities, creativity and productivity are greater (Kim & Shin, 2015).

When a group of individuals share the belief that, through their unified efforts, they can overcome challenges and produce intended results, they are more effective.

There are three core attributes of developing skills and confidence to work in groups, and essential to developing collective student efficacy is the belief that groups can add more value than any individual. For both students and adults, each person in the group needs to have confidence, skills in working in a team, and confidence in the team's overall performance and value for each individual. When this comes together, then enhanced outcomes can be the result for each member and for the team.

Contrast this to what occurs in too many classrooms: 90 percent of students sit in groups and work alone. At least half the time (if not more) the teacher is talking. Students are often tasked with "doing" (but not necessarily learning). Sadly, in many classrooms, only 5 percent of the time is devoted to students talking with their peers. Thus, students lack many reasons and experience to have confidence that working together can enhance the outcomes for their projects. Moreover, when they talk to each other, it is often not about the learning, and too often they can reinforce incorrect information in these more private conversations (Nuthall, 2007).

Learning From a Distance

One potential in distance learning is to change these norms and have students talking, interacting with their peers more frequently. Distance learning can also offer students an opportunity to work collectively rather than independently more of the time. But a risk with distance learning is that we replicate some of these problematic aspects of schooling online.

Teacher Collective Efficacy

The research on the power of collective efficacy is convincing; and it is important to note that this research has been around for decades. To proclaim collective teacher efficacy is the "new number one in Visible Learning" is very misleading. In fact, it is not new. To conduct a meta-analysis, many studies need to be done. Rachel Eells (2011) located twenty-six studies on collective teacher efficacy and Norris (2018) found twenty-four studies. When combining the studies from these two meta-analyses, there were thirty-five studies (twelve were cited in each of the meta-analyses) from 1994 to 2013, based on 2,229 unique teachers, with a mean correlation of .54 or d = 1.27. This places collective efficacy in the top five influences of all time (at least at this writing). Our verdict: it's a great idea, worth pursuing.

While collective teacher efficacy may have a very high average effect, this does not mean that there is not still considerable variation in its effect, and that there are not key characteristics or moderators that can influence the magnitude of the effect size. Eells reported the largest effects were for reading and lowest for social studies. Norris found high effects for both reading and mathematics. Norris also found no differences relating to the socioeconomic status of the school, the number of teachers in the study, or whether the study was published or not. It seems the impact of collective teacher efficacy is generally very substantial.

Yes, these meta-analyses relate to teachers, whereas this book extrapolates the core ideas to collective efficacy with students. We need to be similarly mindful about the possible moderators when applying to students. We need to pay attention to the nature of the learning intentions and success criteria (covered in Chapter 6); teaching methods, assignments and activities (Chapter 5); and assessments (Chapter 8), as these can more or less make a difference to the development of student capabilities, confidence, and success in working in groups. As noted before, the major messages from all the high effects in Visible Learning encompass collective efficacy as part of the larger story. These include high expectations, clear and challenging success criteria, critiquing and moderating others about what they mean by growth, high achievement, and sufficient depth of understanding.

It would have been better to have proclaimed not that collective teacher efficacy is the "new number one" but that collective efficacy helps confirm the major messages about what influences student learning. In other words, the entire Visible Learning evidence base, including collective teacher efficacy, implies that impact on student learning is enhanced when teachers work together to

- plan, evaluate, and critique their impact on the learning lives of students;

- hone their expectations for the students;

- elaborate on their notions of "impact"; and

- build collective confidence in their joint capabilities to make the difference.

Learning From a Distance

Each of these impacts on student learning can be accomplished from a distance. Teachers can plan together for their synchronous and asynchronous lessons. In fact, they can share lessons with each other. Why not have the person most passionate about a given book or topic develop interactive videos for all of the students and share them with the team? In addition, through virtual classroom visits, groups of teachers can hone their expectations for students and determine their impact on students' learning. In doing so, they can build their collective efficacy, including the belief that their efforts are resulting in betting outcomes for students.

Importantly, these collective efforts lead to teachers becoming greater risk takers, receptive to new ideas, and more likely to stay in teaching; holding more positive attitudes about students with disabilities and problem students; engaging in deeper implementation of school improvement; maintaining more positive feelings and attitudes about their school and profession; and being more open to trying new approaches to teaching.

This shows the significant influence of teachers in their narrative about the power of working together, knowing when it is optimal to work in groups, when alone, and when with other teachers. It shows the importance of leaders creating high trust for teachers to safely critique, explore and evaluate each other's learning; ensuring all are prepared and involved in the team learning; and celebrating joint ownership of the successes from the collective impact. The aim is to develop school cultures characterized by high expectations for student success, a shared language that represents a focus on *learning* as opposed to *teaching*, a shared belief that success and failure in student learning is more about what they as teachers do or do not do, and a shared value in solving problems of practice together. We will be applying these messages to develop the case for collective student efficacy.

Some teachers (and students) may not agree, may not want to be involved, prefer to just do their teaching and learning their way by themselves, and some, quite frankly, are not that social at all in the staff or classroom. This means that they have little confidence in benefiting from working in a collective. In groups, there can be social loafing, negativity, and cliques can form. Without acknowledgment, feedback, and involvement, there can be manipulation, passive-aggressive behaviors, and sabotage for personal gain. There can be lack of engagement and complacency. Groups can engage in talk, talk, talk that is contrived. Andy Hargreaves (2001) has long reminded us of contrived collegiality—that which is administratively regulated, compulsory, implementation-oriented, fixed in time and space, and predictable. There can be competing factions within a team. And we have all heard "but that is not how we do it here." There are so many barriers to teams being successful. Do not assume that because you have a collective, you necessarily have a positive and powerful process for improvement. But when it works, it's exceptionally powerful.

This book, however, is not about collective teacher efficacy (powerful as it can be); rather, it is about translating these powerful messages into *collective student efficacy*. Yes, there is no meta-analysis demonstrating the power of collective student efficacy, but there are many related findings that build a very strong case for advocating and writing about this notion, and we hope that this book will inspire more research on this topic. Take, for example, the evidence about collaborative learning. There are forty-eight meta-analyses relating to cooperative and collaborative learning, based on over 4,000 studies of half a million students, with an average effect

VISIBLE LEARNING® BAROMETER

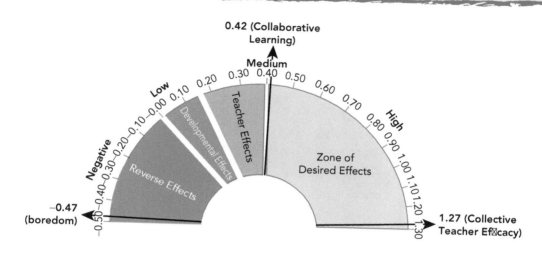

Figure 2.1

size of .42 (se = .12) and ranked 139 out of three hundred influences (see www.VISIBLELEARNINGMetaX.com). Thus, collaborative learning is one of the favorable interventions, but much more could be done to improve this overall effect. If the wisdom of the crowd is correct, then why doesn't collaborative learning have an effect size similar to collective teacher efficacy? Our verdict? Collaborative learning is a great starting idea, but much more is needed. Figure 2.1 shows the effect sizes for both collaborative learning and collective teacher efficacy on the Visible Learning barometer. Collective student efficacy is much more, though built on, the findings about cooperative and collaborative thinking. Hence, the focus of this book.

This book aims to identify WHEN collective efficacy is powerful for students, HOW to create the conditions to maximize the benefits of collective efficacy, and WHAT attributes of tasks are most conducive to working collectively. It takes the large corpus of Visible Learning research and reframes many of the claims about the student influences, showing the remarkable power of teaching students to have high confidence and skills working in teams.

Collective Student Efficacy

Considering all of the above research on teachers' collective efficacy and its demonstrated impact, we couldn't help but wonder if students' collective efficacy would have the same positive impact on their learning. Using the claims from Bandura and others, and from the work on collective teacher efficacy, we suggest that collective student efficacy has the potential to accelerate learning. To do so, each student needs to have

- confidence about their ability to successfully contribute to a task or accomplish an activity as part of a team;
- skills in working for himself or herself and working with all in a team; and
- a shared belief in the team's collective capabilities to organize and execute the optimal course of action.

To harness the power of collective student efficacy, it is thus critical to investigate the skills, motivations, and dispositions of the student. It is also important to consider the tasks, assessments, success criteria, and teaching methods enacted by the teacher.

We also need to make a major declaration about what collective student efficacy is NOT. We are not talking about collaborative grouping, cooperative learning, or merely rearranging desks such that students sit in groups. We are not talking about students working toward a common goal or working on different parts of a problem and simply piecing the solutions together. Some forms of traditional group work even mitigate against collective efficacy.

Those who have defended cooperative learning have hinted at the importance of developing collective efficacy. For example, Johnson and Johnson (2009) proposed five essential elements of cooperative learning:

1. There exists positive interdependence among the members in terms of goals, rewards, resources, roles, and tasks.

2. Every member has the sense of individual and group accountability.

3. There are promotive interactions among members (e.g., encourage one another).

4. Members use appropriate social skills (e.g., communicate accurately and clearly).

5. Group members conduct group processing by reflecting on their past cooperative actions and decide how to move forward.

While these five apply to developing collective efficacy, they did not specifically highlight the importance of developing collective efficacy as the core notion leading to the power of the group, enhancing the confidence to successfully contribute to the group, or having confidence that the group could produce better outcomes than each individual.

To accomplish collective student efficacy, there are various skills we identify. We have grouped them into the "I" and "We" skills. Both are necessary for collective student efficacy to flourish and ensure better learning.

The "I" Skills

The "I" skills are based on individual self-efficacy to contribute to the collective, to the belief that the group can enhance the outcomes, and to group confidence to undertake a task. "I" skills are dependent on the Goldilocks principle—not so much confidence that often leads to under-performance (Dunlosky & Rawson, 2012), frequently because the over-confident student is resistant to the ideas of others, believing instead that his or her path is the only correct one. And not too under-confident, when learners doubt that they possess the internal resources such as ability and perseverance and question the usefulness of external resources (teacher guidance, materials) to complete the task (Stirin et al., 2012). Learners who have a well-calibrated, "just right" level of self-confidence are socially aware of others but don't spend a lot of time in social comparisons (Maclellan, 2014). We also note that students' collective efficacy beliefs seem to be positively, though weakly, associated to their individual efficacy beliefs (Pina-Neves et al., 2013), so we should not confuse high levels of individual confidence with confidence to then work in groups.

Learners who have a well-calibrated, "just right" level of self-confidence are socially aware of others but don't spend a lot of time in social comparisons (Maclellan, 2014).

Other important "I" skills include seeing oneself as a learner and not being constrained by beliefs about whether one is a high or low achiever. It is the willingness to learn regardless of prior achievement that matters most. It is being resilient in facing and embracing challenge and understanding that failure is potentially an opportunity to learn. It is being aware of one's own ability to individually perform tasks in the group and the skills to share task perceptions and share goals (Panadero & Järvellä, 2015).

Each member of a high performing group shares monitoring of their progress and adapts their performance in light of this evaluating; that is, they learn to be assessment capable and prepared to evaluate their processes and impact. They also share group motivational efforts and emotional regulation. There are individual skills in working with a group to plan goals, decide how to follow directions, divide up task components, establish strategies to overcome challenges, share or clarify information, and maintain on-task behavior. There are skills when evaluating the achievements of individuals and the group, when providing explanations, identifying challenges, and deciding on adaptions to maximize reaching the success criteria (Pandaro et al., 2015). When individuals in groups are able to focus on monitoring their content understanding rather than the task or behavior, it seems to afford the opportunity to develop deeper understanding (Rogat & Linnenbrink-Garcia, 2011).

Learning From a Distance

Distance learning cannot be seen as a list of tasks to complete. When that happens, students focus on task completion and not their individual and collective learning. Instead, groups should focus on their level of understanding and periodically review their progress. For example, they might use a four-level system to assess their collective understanding with the following criteria:

1) We can explain our success and are ready to teach others;

2) We own our learning and can work collaboratively to extend our understanding;

3) We are making progress and need more practice;

4) We are beginning our learning journey and need more help.

This regulation can lead to conflict and disruption, so the "I" skills of conflict resolution, negotiation, and communication skills can help lead the group to success. Students may need to be taught to recognize and encourage desirable and discourage undesirable team conflict, listen non-evaluatively and use active listening skills, recognize and interpret nonverbal messages in the collective, seek, listen, and understand feedback to and from others, and develop the outward skills of communication (e.g., eye contact, nonverbal, gestural, and body language skills, paralanguage) as well as active listening skills. These include being attentive, asking related questions, requesting clarification, noticing the emotions of others, and being able to summarize and restate. In addition, effective communicators are able to clearly explain, provide evidence, gain and yield the floor, and move the group forward in its task.

The "We" Skills

Certain "We" skills (skills the entire group shares) are also necessary for collective efficacy to occur, especially social sensitivity. That is, can students stand in another's shoes and see the world

> ### "I" Skills
>
> - A "just right" level of self-confidence in my own ability to contribute to the group
> - Seeing myself as a learner
> - Setting group goals
> - Working together while following directions and delegating tasks
> - Identifying challenges and overcoming obstacles
> - Verbal communication skills (conflict resolution, negotiation, desirable argumentation)
> - Nonverbal communication skills (eye contact, gestures, body language, facial expressions, tone)

from their perspective? This involves the ability to acknowledge mistakes, accept others as they are, decode and understand what others are thinking and feeling, become social problem solvers, empathize with others and the group's moods and feelings, and listen and demonstrate they have listened to others in the group (Bender et al., 2012). If students do not have this "we" skill of social sensitivity, then we as teachers need to teach these skills as they are critical to students' future success when working in groups. In addition, there are several "we" skills that derive from social sensitivity that are necessary to ensure success.

Potency. The skills of believing "we will succeed" in this group is called potency. The concept of group potency was proposed by Shea and Guzzo (1987) to be a key determinant of team effectiveness. The higher the potency among the group members, the more positive the collective outcomes. This is why turn-taking in a group is so important. Turn-taking involves anticipating the other person's pauses and avoiding overlap. The flow is higher when the student is actively listening and making predictions about when the speaker will end and the next speech utterances, allowing the listener to decide when to speak and what to say next (Holler et al., 2016), begin.

There are many skills, or lack of, that can cause barriers to success, including social loafing, not agreeing to rules of conduct, not establishing individual accountability, not encouraging group loyalty, not evaluating progress, and not dealing with conflict, nonparticipation, withdrawal, scapegoating, bullying, irregular attendance, aggressive behavior, or arguments. Perhaps the strongest among these barriers is social loafing. Social loafing occurs when individuals in the group reduce their motivation and effort to work collectively compared with when they work individually. Students who participate in social loafing expect their efforts to be less likely to lead to valuable outcomes when working collectively. They sit back and contribute little but then gain benefit from the collective work of the others in the groups. Karau and Williams (1993) conducted a meta-analysis on social loafing based on seventy-eight studies. They found an effect size of -.44, which is a quite substantial negative influence on group outcomes. This indicates that students worked harder alone (or in the presence of others but their work is not combined with the inputs of others) than collectively.

Learning From a Distance

Social loafing can happen in distance learning as well. As we will see later in this book, task design is an important preventative measure that teachers can use. In addition, inviting reflection from students about their level of engagement can provide students an opportunity to recognize their lack of efforts and encourage them to engage. Importantly, asking students to report on their peers' level of engagement can backfire and reduce the collective efficacy of a group.

"We" Skills

- Social sensitivity (empathy, acknowledging mistakes, accepting others)
- Potency
- Motivation to tackle the task together
- Ability to take turns
- Flexibility in taking on roles within the group or team
- Determination to succeed together
- Collective responsibility for keeping going and meeting deadlines
- A sense of group responsibility for each other as equal participants
- Being able to give supportive feedback to each other without diminishing self-efficacy

Social loafing is more likely to occur when individual outputs cannot be or are not evaluated collectively when working on tasks that are perceived low in meaningfulness or personal involvement, when group-level comparison standards are not available, when working with strangers, when their inputs to the collective outcome are reduced with those of other group members, and when their inputs to the collective outcome are redundant with those of other group members.

Throughout this book we will return to these "I" and "We" skills both in terms of the role of the teacher to instill these skills and also in terms of how to create tasks, conditions, and evaluations that allow the students to develop these skills. We recommend this teaching and learning within the content of various curricula area, rather than developing as a separate set of skills. So much of the current debate about 21st century skills such as collaborative problem solving is divorced from the development of these skills within appropriate tasks in current curricula domains. There is much evidence that teaching these skills in a generic manner does not transfer to being used successfully within various curricula domains.

The Role of the Teacher in Collective Student Efficacy

Throughout the chapters that follow, we focus on the role of the teachers and the students. It is the teacher who has the power to choose the tasks, assessments, success criteria, and optimal teaching strategies. We start by discussing the nature of collective and individual success criteria and some optimal ways to set up groups and establish appropriate roles for team members. We then move to the nature of the tasks for collective student efficacy. Not all tasks are appropriate for groups, and those that have the highest task interdependence (encouraging coordination, communication, and cooperation among students) maximize the development of collective efficacy (Gully et al., 2002; Katz-Navon & Erez, 2005). We use prior research (Steiner, 1972) to distinguish between different types of interdependent tasks: additive, compensatory, conjunctive, and discretionary.

The tasks need to be appropriately challenging (not too hard, not too easy, not too boring), and be conducted in a safe culture where errors and mistakes by individuals and the group are seen as opportunities to learn and where there is respect for others' views, skills, and judgments. There needs to be attention to the motivational aspects when initiating, undertaking, and completing the task, and there needs to be maximal formative feedback from the teacher and group members.

There is no point asking students to work collectively, then grade them individually. But giving a collective grade also has problems, and we have already noted the problems of social loafing in groups. Why should social loafers get the benefit of grades earned by the committed and contributing members to a group task? The aim is for all members to experience and enthuse over collective success and to develop their content and social knowledge in this process of undertaking and completing tasks.

The Role of the Student in Collective Efficacy

From the early years, children learn to live, work, and play in groups. They come to many learning tasks with some collaborative skills or, in some cases, a dislike of working with others. We start by looking at the cycle of skill development, leading to a longer discussion about the "I" and "we" skills that students need to develop to effectively develop their collective efficacy.

The art of the science of teaching is knowing what is appropriately challenging for each student, given their previous experiences and successes in learning.

It is most worthwhile to refer back to the individual self-efficacy work, pioneered by Albert Bandura (Bandura & Walters, 1977). This is a student's belief in his or her capacity to execute actions necessary to produce specific outcomes. Confidence to exert control over one's motivation, behavior, and social environment. The beauty of this notion is that it can be taught, it can be positively impacted by wise choices of appropriately challenging tasks, and it can be influenced by feedback to the student. Note, a key word in this last sentence, is "appropriately," as if the work is too easy, it can be seen as boring, and if too hard, it can be not worth the investment to complete the work or achieve the success criteria. The art of the science of teaching is knowing what is appropriately challenging for each student, given their previous experiences and successes in learning.

Nearly every student has a sense of confidence about their work, their learning, and themselves. Agency goes one step further, as it relates to a student's capacity to take action and shape one's destiny. Agency is dynamic as it ebbs and flows, is situational depending on the task, and it can be taught, often by allowing a gradual release of their agency from the teacher to the students. We outline one of the major instances when confidence and agency become critical—when there are errors, mistakes, confusion, and misunderstanding. Some students see errors as reinforcement for them not knowing, feeling stupid, and not being a successful learner. Others see errors as worthwhile challenges, as opportunities for new learning, and as indicators they are not there yet. Here is where notions of resilience, growth mindsets, and coping strategies become critical.

When working in groups, there are critical communication skills, including being attentive, asking related questions, requesting clarification, noticing the emotions of others, being able to summarize and restate, clearly explaining, providing evidence, gaining and yielding the floor, taking turns, and moving the group forward in its task. We identify turn-taking as one of the highest correlates of successful collective group work. Consider your classes and ask whether there is a high incidence of turn-taking. Or consider having someone come into your class or watch a group in action and map the turn-taking. We learn from a very early age to take turns in conversations, and some become better at this skill than others. The skills include learning how to get and maintain attention with others, establishing common ground, making repairs when we are misunderstood, and deciding what is relevant to contribute. As children engage in turn-taking, their contributions can be irrelevant (too long or too short), some choose not to take turns, and some are more prepared to engage in turn-taking with others (including adults and peers) they know and trust. Building their skills in turn-taking and contributing to the group is very much a function of the updates and feedback they get from others in the conversations.

Learning From a Distance

One of the ways that you can increase turn-taking is to structure tasks and assign roles. For example, a group of teachers developed roles for breakout rooms that included the following: **Host** – Communicate with the instructor and share any questions or concerns the group may have; **Facilitator** – Invite people to share and monitor the turns each person takes; **Recorder** – Take notes in the breakout room as people share, making sure to include names as people share; **Reporter** – Summarize the group's response and share with the whole class.

We comment on the role and development of "we" skills and explore the criticality of developing social sensitivity of others (indeed a core skill for successful turn-taking conversations). Here's the good news: Social sensitivity can be taught, nurtured, and developed, and we outline some processes for teaching this skill. As well, there is the group's confidence it can be effective—it can have potency—which also can and needs to be taught.

CHAPTER 3

DEVELOPING THE "I" SKILLS

It is a few weeks into the school year and Jessica Lowe's students have been studying rhetoric as part of their English class. They have analyzed a number of popular press articles, noting the ways in which authors use logic, emotions, and ethics to support their ideas. At first, they read the texts individually and engage in whole class discussions. Over time, Ms. Lowe invites students to analyze the texts using a graphic organizer designed to capture the rhetorical devices. They also respond in writing to the prompts Ms. Lowe assigned. But Ms. Lowe knows that this is not the end goal for her class. She is getting to know her students and their learning needs. And she is planning to assign tasks that require that they engage with their peers.

To introduce this shift, she has hung posters around the room that say, "Qualities or behaviors I believe create a positive learning space are . . . " As Ms. Lowe says, "They have to learn how to learn in groups. And they have to learn to develop as a collective if they are going to learn in those types of situations." The students are asked to identify qualities and behaviors that they believe will foster a good learning environment. Ms. Lowe keeps an updated list on her computer as her students discuss the prompt and record their responses on the posters. There are over one hundred different responses collected. When students finish recording their ideas on paper, Ms. Lowe shares the list on a Google form and students are invited to vote on the top behaviors that will be learned and practiced in their class. We will focus on her first period class. The students select the following:

- Share your ideas (they will add to others' thoughts).

- Ask for help when you need it; help others when they need it.

- Be supportive, have positive energy, and give off good vibes.

- Do not forget to ADVOCATE for yourself and others when you need help or clarification.

The risk with a list like this is that it can become platitudes rather than a set of guiding principles that help students learn. Ms. Lowe knows that and attempts to counter it by creating both experiences and tools that her students can use to develop their collective efficacy. As we have noted, collective efficacy capitalizes on the power of students coming together to learn, believing that they can and will learn, setting and monitoring goals, and engaging in learning tasks together. Of course, not all learning is done in the collective. There are some tasks that students complete on their own. After all, our aim is to create independent and interdependent learners, not dependent learners.

Back to Ms. Lowe's classroom. The week following the development of their norms, Ms. Lowe introduced students to a self-assessment tool she developed that focused on two of the five points her students wanted to develop, namely sharing ideas, and asking for advice or feedback. She said to them, "I was thinking about our agreements and our collective desire to learn from each other, so I put together a draft of some points that we might want to consider when we talk with our groups today. It is only a draft, and I hope that we can improve it over the next week. Notice that I left spaces at the bottom to add other indicators. Please take a few minutes to read through the statements and give them some thought before we engage in our reading today." The room went quiet as the students started to read the items on the tool. As students started to look up, Ms. Lowe said,

> Now to our task for today. We are still learning about
> rhetorical devices and how to analyze texts for those devices.
> I've selected a fairly difficult task. It's actually from your
> history class. You'll get a jump on this because you're going
> to read this same text for another reason later this week
> in history. Anyway, the text is called "A Declaration of
> Conscience" and was delivered by Margaret Chase Smith in
> the US Senate on June 1, 1950 in response to Senator Joseph
> McCarthy's claim to possess the names of 205 'card-carrying
> communists' in the State Department. You'll learn more about
> this history later this week. Our focus is on Senator Smith's
> use of rhetoric.

Ms. Lowe distributed the reading and turned her attention to the discussion protocol that she had selected. The students were expected to discuss the following:

- What **Assumptions** does the author of the text hold?

- What do you **Agree** with in the text?

- What do you want to **Argue** with in the text?

- What parts of the text do you **Aspire** to?

Learning From a Distance

The 4 A's protocol works well in distance learning. Students can read the text in the main room and then move to breakout rooms to engage in this type of discussion. The structure increases the likelihood that students will successfully complete the task. Ideally, they would have been introduced to the protocol via a video that was part of their asynchronous learning. Try to reserve synchronous learning for student interaction, providing feedback, and guiding students' thinking.

As Ms. Lowe said, "First, we'll engage in a discussion so we know that we understand what's happening in the text. We'll use the 4 A's protocol that you used before (Assumptions, Agree, Argue, Aspire). Once we understand the text, we'll examine it again for the rhetorical devices used. Are you ready to read and discuss?" The students nod and get to work. Listening in to some of the groups reveals varied levels of collective student efficacy. For example, in one group, Omar has shared his ideas and now Asha is sharing hers. There was no interaction between them; they simply took turns sharing their own answers. The members of Omar's group are not taking notes while others speak. Instead, they seem to be waiting for their turn.

In another group, Kasim has just suggested to the group that he believes that the senator thinks the United States is going to end up destroying itself. He says, "I think it's a fair assumption to say that the senator is worried about her country. She thinks that the fear of communists could make Americans give up on values that they believe in." Before he could finish, Justine says, "I'm not sure I agree. I mean, I see how she starts by shocking everyone with an emotional appeal saying that we will have a 'national suicide,' but I don't think that people are going to give up on their values because of one senator."

The conversation continues as the group works to make sense of text. They are sharing their ideas, listening to others, changing their opinions as a result of their interactions, and deepening their understanding. They are on the path to collective student efficacy, but only a few steps in. Our role in this book is to shine a light on the path and provide ways that you can build collective efficacy with your students. You may not teach English, but the ideas contained in this book transcend grade levels and content areas. We are calling for a change in how teachers see students, the tasks and opportunities provided for them, and the outcomes we value in this place called school. Notice that the students in Ms. Lowe's class used both individual and collective skills in completing their work. This is an important notion and one that requires some additional explanation.

We can use this example of Ms. Lowe's class to introduce some of the "I" skills needed to be successful as individuals and the collective. They include these areas:

- Knowledge building: The record of the students' ideas and the self-assessment tool, which serves as a diagnosis to see what students knew or did not know before they went into their groups

- Self-efficacy: Being supportive, having positive energy, and giving off good vibes

- Appropriately challenging goals

- Receiving and giving feedback

- Agency: Advocating for yourself and others when you/they need help or clarification

- Resilience: Identifying what you do not know, willingness to listen to other and new ideas, perseverance in redoing and practice

- Communication skills: Asking for help when you need it; helping others when they need it as well as listening and taking turns

Knowledge Building

In Ms. Lowe's class, the students engaged in a task that required them to analyze a complex text from the past. None of them had seen the text before, but they had a lot of background knowledge about the time period in which this text was written, as well as the government system operating in the United States. As students interacted in their groups, they negotiated the meaning of the text and their understanding of the text, or their appreciation of the text, increased because of the interactions.

Learning From a Distance

The number of minutes we have in physical school are constrained by schedules. In distance learning, we can assign different amounts and types of background building tasks, based on what students already know and still need to know. Most learning management systems allow teachers to deploy content differently based on student needs. For example, one student might need to view one interactive video on a topic whereas another might need three to close the knowledge gap.

Too often, not attending to the students' knowledge building before they venture into group work is the major barrier to the success of the collective. We note in Chapter 5 that many problem-based lessons (PBL) fail because the students have insufficient background knowledge to apply, understand, or be involved in the problem phase. For example, the effect-size of PBL increases from .15 to .50 when it is established that the students have sufficient background knowledge to move to the PBL phase. Again, the whole point of collective student efficacy is to ensure each student develops confidence about their ability and disposition to successfully contribute to a task or accomplish an activity as part of a team and to develop a shared belief in a collective's capabilities to organize and execute the courses of action.

This knowledge building can occur in a group, and for a good illustration of this, we again use the Jigsaw method. Commonly in the first round of the Jigsaw, students are assigned tasks that help them build the knowledge base, learn the vocabulary of the task, and understand and decode the problem that is to be addressed. They can do this in groups, provided the teacher is confident that there is a necessary baseline of knowledge before moving to the deeper tasks of building relations or transferring to other situations.

Self-efficacy

The starting place is individual self-efficacy. Bandura (1986, 1997) proposed that self-efficacy is an individual's belief in his or her capacity to execute actions necessary to produce specific outcomes. In part, it is the confidence an individual has in his or her ability to exert control over one's own motivation, behavior, and social environment. Of course, this can go too far. A student who is overconfident actually performs less well. Dunlosky and Rawson (2012) suggest that this is because an overconfident student is resistant to the ideas of others, believing instead that his or her path is the correct one. This contrasts with under-confident learners who doubt that they possess the internal resources (such as ability) necessary to accomplish the task or produce the outcome. Under-confident learners also question the usefulness of external resources (teacher guidance, materials) to complete the task (Stirin et al., 2012). Thus, the challenge lies in ensuring students have a healthy and accurate understanding of their efficacy.

As Bandura noted, self-efficacy is influenced by one's experience, observation, persuasion, and emotion. For example, success on a particular type of writing task increases the likelihood that the student's self-efficacy is increased and that this student approaches the next writing task with more confidence and even enthusiasm.

The major motivator for developing individual self-efficacy includes the enactive learning experience, experiences which allow the student to focus on their personal accomplishments and which are subject to mastery or evaluative criteria. Our confidence can be enhanced

- when credible and trustworthy people (e.g., teachers, parents, peers) in any collective attribute success to the student [and in the case of the collective to the student_s_];
- when a student observes another person complete the task and comes to see that he or she is also capable of the same;
- when students feel excitement and satisfaction from mastery;
- where challenging expectations are realized (but less so when non-challenging expectations are met);
- when social persuasion of others helps nudge students toward mastery; and
- when it is "normal here" to invest, learn from failures and errors, and others are seen to be having similar pathways of success and failure leading to mastery.

Success breeds confidence, help from others breeds confidence, and enjoyment in learning breeds confidence.

Success breeds confidence, help from others breeds confidence, and enjoyment in learning breeds confidence.

These enactive learning experiences are powerful, sustained, and remain significant over time (Phan & Ngu, 2016). This means we need to encourage students to enjoy and appreciate their learning, give them feedback relative to where they are currently in their learning, ensure that the learning has meaning and personal relevance to the learner, and be clear with them about what it means to be successful (feedback thus helps fill this gap). While doing so, we need to ensure that the experience is nonthreatening, welcomed, and engenders a sense of engagement and feelings of self-value.

Not surprisingly, individual self-efficacy is an important contributor to collective efficacy. If a student believes that she knows the necessary processes and has worthwhile knowledge and background information, that student is much more likely to engage with the collective. Further, self-efficacy is a by-product of collective efficacy. When that student experiences success in the collective, she tells herself that her contributions were valuable and that her efforts were worth the investment. In this way, self-efficacy grows through the experiences students have with others. Students' collective efficacy beliefs are positively associated to their individual efficacy beliefs (Pina-Neves et al., 2013).

As educators, there are several ways that we can build students' self-efficacy. Piles of books and Internet sites provide good information about this, so we will not spend too much time on it as we are more focused on collective efficacy. However, we recognize that collective efficacy and self-efficacy are connected and mutually reinforcing. As we have noted, the experience of success, succeeding in accomplishing tasks, is the most important source of self-efficacy. Christensen, the author of *The Innovator's Dilemma*, wrote with coauthors Allworth and Dillon a book titled *How Will You Measure Your Life?* (2012). As these business professionals note: "Going to school is not a job that children are trying to get done. The two fundamental jobs that children need to do are to feel successful and to have friends—every day" (p. 111). They continue, reminding us that students do not need schools to get these jobs done. They can join a gang or get hired at a fast-food restaurant. They concluded by saying that "schools are structured to help most students feel like failures" (p. 111). Of course, we want the opposite—to teach students that they can be successful, and particularly they can be successful with others.

Appropriately Challenging Goals

Learning increases when the teacher and students understand the learning goals. In fact, the effect size of learning goals versus no goals is .51. But the type of goal matters. Goals cannot be too easily accomplished as they will be boring for students. And they cannot be so complicated that students will fail to reach them in a reasonable amount of time. Remember success breeds motivation. Thus, appropriately challenging goals are important, and the effect size is .59. Learning tasks need to be aligned with the learning goals. Tasks need to be structured so that students understand what is being asked of them and how they know that they are being successful. When teachers provide students with progress monitoring tools, students can experience approximations of success and potentially build their self-efficacy. For example, the students in Isaac Stevens' third grade class were learning about the states of matter. Mr. Stevens let his students know that they would be learning about three states of matter. He asked, "How many states of matter are we learning about?" The students responded in unison, "Three!" Then Mr. Stevens said, "Please turn to your partner and tell your partner how many states of matter we're learning about." The students did so. Mr. Stevens responded, "See, you already learned something. You already know that there are three states of matter. But we need to know what matter is and what a state is. It is not like Texas or Florida. It's a different use of the word. I've created a checklist for you to monitor your own learning. When you are sure about one of these, check with your partner and then plan a time to show me what you've learned."

Learning From a Distance

The chat feature is an effective way for students to rapidly experience success. Had Mr. Stevens been teaching from a distance, he could have asked students to type their response in the chat and on the count of three hit send. This provides some nice wait time and prevents students from copying the first person to respond.

Some of the items on the checklist included:

- I can name the three states: solids, liquid, and gas.
- I can describe the properties of the solid state.
- I know how heat can change the states.

In his case, the checklist served as a way for students to experience intermittent success rather than waiting until the end of the unit when they engaged in a lab. Of course, there are other ways for students to monitor their progress. Our point is that these types of tools can help students experience success.

In addition to experiencing success, peer models can foster self-efficacy and the willingness to take on challenging work, especially when students see their peers struggle and work through a concept or idea. There are two types of peer models: coping and mastery. The coping model outlines the students' beliefs about their ability to cope with external stressors and challenges in completing tasks. The focus is more on their coping strategies than on the stressor itself. Working in groups, for example, can be a stressor but what is more salient is whether the student believes they have the coping strategies such that they will invest effort and persist in the face of what they see as barriers (their own or others' barriers). Attending to the coping strategies is much more effective at building the self-efficacy of peers to work with classmates. As the teacher prompts, and the students experience success, they can come to understand that they can accomplish and master similar things.

Up until the 1970–80s, researchers studied stress in children and focused on many ways to reduce the stressors in children's lives. The success rates were low as they were attending to the wrong issue. Since this time, the preponderance of attention has switched to the coping strategies we have and how we can develop strategies to deal with stressors. A student in the above example may know no forms of matter, so they could distance themselves from the task, or they could problem solve, or they could self-blame for not knowing. There are many different ways of coping with the same stressor. Our role as teachers is to teach optimal coping strategies when students do not know, when they feel threatened, when they are working with others, or when they are off task. There are three major types of coping strategies:

1. Cognitive strategies, such as seeking social support, humor, problem-solving, positive reinterpretation, persistence;

2. Emotional strategies, such as relaxation, denial, venting, self-blame;

3. Avoidance strategies, such as distancing, disengaging, internalizing, externalizing, downsizing expectations, inappropriate behavior, and distracting.

The cognitive strategies are usually the most effective, but some of the emotional strategies can help lead them toward the cognitive strategies. We certainly need to recognize and engage in reteaching when we see avoidance strategies both at the individual and at the collective level.

For example, listen to the students in Brian Duffy's math class as they think aloud when working on problems with algebraic exponents. Ibrahim offered to model how to solve the first problem, which read:

$$2^{(2x+4)} = 8^{(x+1)}$$

As he approached the dry erase board, Ibrahim said, "This is harder than I thought. I was going to divide 8 by 2, but now I'm thinking that will leave me with 1 on the left and 4 on the right, so that isn't really going to help. I need to do something else. Let me think."

After waiting several seconds, Mr. Duffy says, "What I remember about these problems, and we haven't done a lot of them yet this year, but what I remember is that you have to **factor** to get the bases to be equal before you can deal with the exponents." He used his voice to focus on the word factor.

Ibrahim responded, "Oh, I can factor. I can change the 8 to $2 \bullet 2 \bullet 2$ or 2^3. And when I do that, I don't have to do anything to the other side. Now let me think about how that helps."

Stephanie asks Ibrahim if she can give him a hint, saying, "I think I have an idea if you want me to tell you." Ibrahim says yes and Stephanie responds, "Remember when Mr. Duffy said that if you make the bases equal then you only have to worry about the exponents, or something like that? So, leave the left alone and carry the 3 through the exponent. Make sense?"

Ibrahim does so, creating the following:

$$2^{(2x+4)} = 2^{(3x+3)}$$

He says, "So, I think we got it now. Because the bases are now equal, I can just deal with the exponents. And now it's just moving things around, like minus three from both sides leave 1 on the left and minus 2x from both sides leaves x on the right, so x=1. Bam."

Learning From a Distance

This lesson could have been conducted using the shared whiteboard feature in a virtual meeting room. The moves from the teacher would essentially be the same. Students can use the annotation tools to share their thinking. The addition, in distance learning, would be that the peers would not just be listening. They could use the chat and the reaction buttons to engage with the lesson.

Mr. Duffy adds, "Exactly. I appreciate your thinking, Ibrahim, and your support, Stephanie. So, we learned something valuable here. We need to first try to make the bases equal so that we can solve the problem. I have another one for you to try, but this time the bases are already equal. Oops, maybe I shouldn't have said that. Let's try." The lesson continues as students work through various examples based on the model that Ibrahim (and Stephanie) provided.

When Mr. Duffy approached Marco, who appeared to be struggling with one of the problems, Marco looked up and said, "Don't help me yet. Ibrahim factored first and so did I, but it's not working. When I solve for x, it doesn't make sense. [pause] Oh, wait, I didn't apply the 2 through the equation. I missed that step. Come back and check me later." Marco used ideas from the modeling he experienced, but even more importantly, he believed that he could solve the problem and persevered through it: self-efficacy at its best.

Teachers can build and reinforce students' self-efficacy to take on challenging tasks through setting appropriate goals and providing feedback. Goals are an interesting phenomenon and it is important we make them not too hard, not too easy, and not too boring. Graham Nuthall (2007) argued that about 50 percent of what is taught in every class is already known by the students, and while some children (especially early elementary students) are compliant and will do whatever we ask, many come to only want to be engaged in the challenge if the task meets the Goldilocks' principle—not too easy, not too hard, and not too boring.

We believe that students can set appropriately challenging goals or become committed to your challenging goals, as accomplishing goals you are committed to is rewarding. For example, the students in Miko Haji's art class established goals for themselves related to the types of pieces they would produce for an upcoming show. Andrew's goal was to "have five paintings that showed different uses of light" whereas Marisa's goal was to "create a self-portrait that had the correct proportions and perspective."

But we also know that teachers need to establish goals for students because these goals communicate to students that you believe that they can achieve at a high level. In Martha Ramirez's fourth grade class, every student knows their current reading level. In addition to the instruction she provides, the school uses a tool that assesses students' reading performance as they complete online tasks that provide practice with texts at the students' current reading level. Ms. Ramirez has a goal that all of her students read at least at an 850 Lexile level. This is a performance goal that Ms. Ramirez publicly shares. She has private conversations with her students about their current reading levels and how they can improve their ability to read and understand texts. With her students, she focuses more on mastery goals.

Eva, for example, reads at the 650 Lexile level. During a recent conference, Ms. Ramirez said to Eva, "Your reading level has increased by 50 points in the past month. I hope you are feeling really good about that. You are a great learner. What have you been doing that made the difference?"

Eva responded that she was slowing down a little bit and trying to really focus on the meanings. As she said, "My goal was to not rush just to get done with the reading. I sometimes have to read the part again to understand but now I am paying attention to what it says."

Ms. Ramirez responded, "That is great to hear. Your strategies are paying off. I think it's time to change your goal a little bit. You have accomplished this goal and now it's one of your habits. I think it's time to focus on words and what they mean. I would like you to identify five words from every text you read and talk about those words with other people. It could be your friends or your family or people in the afterschool program. Your new goal is to increase your vocabulary. Can you do it?"

Eva responds, "Yes! I can do it. Do you want me to show you the words?" Ms. Ramirez answered, "Yes, I would love that. You know how much I love words. It will be fun to share words with you, just the two of us having a list."

When she met with Daveon, Ms. Ramirez said, "You're reading at the 900 Lexile level. Well done. You have increased your reading volume like we discussed. And now, you have exceeded my class goal, but you know that you're not done learning to read, right? [Daveon nods] Fourth and fifth grade go all the way to 1010 Lexile and then you can start reading at the middle school level. Your goal is different. I want you to start summarizing what you have read in your notebook. And then, when you've read three or four texts that are related, I'd like you to put it all together. I'm thinking that you could record your ideas about the texts and how they fit together and submit it so that I can listen on my way home from school. Then, each week, we could talk about your thinking about the different texts you have read. Does that sound like a plan for the next couple of weeks?"

Learning From a Distance

Practice is an important part of learning and is critical in distance learning if instruction has a chance of sticking. One potential for distance learning is varied amounts of practice that allow students to achieve their goals. For example, if a student wanted to increase her understanding of informational texts, she could read a lot more of them, write Amazon reviews, develop Flipgrid presentations for her peers, teach members of her family, and use the monitoring tools that her teacher provides her. Of course, she could still join in the synchronous lessons, but her teacher could monitor her learning based on the goal she had for herself. Her teacher could also schedule office hours with the student to have the same type of conversation that Daveon had with Ms. Ramirez.

Daveon agreed and said, "You know, I didn't like reading when I was in second grade. I felt stupid all the time. I don't know what happened, but now it just works. It's sick, all the information out there that you can learn. For this week, I am deciding between the new tombs with gold in Greece or the statues on Easter Island. Which one do you want to know about?"

In both cases, the goals that Ms. Ramirez developed for her students fostered their self-efficacy. Notice that she attributed their success to their efforts and noted that they accomplished what they set out to do. Together, goals, modeling, and experiencing success can build the self-efficacy skills that are so necessary for students to find school rewarding and for them to engage with their peers in collectives.

Receiving and Giving Feedback

There is so much discussion about the best ways to give feedback, admonitions to give lots of feedback, and debates about whether it is best to give grades or comments. The problem is that feedback is one of the more variable influences we know of—the same feedback today can work but when repeated tomorrow does not. About one-third of all feedback can have a negative impact, and even including praise with feedback about the task can dilute the impact. We have spent a lot of time trying to understand how to increase the power of feedback, because when effective, it is among the more powerful influences of all. Consider five findings from the Visible Learning research:

1. Feedback is more powerful when it includes information about "where to next" on the basis of feedback about "where am I going" and "how am I going."

2. Feedback needs to be focused at the level of instructional cycle as it moves from knowing what surface), to knowing how (deep), to transfer; or to task, process, and self-regulation.

3. Feedback is only as good as it is received, interpreted, and acted on.

4. Feedback to the teacher about his or her impact is not only among the most powerful influences on student learning but sets up the modeling for students to be receptive to, welcome, and interpret feedback.

5. Feedback from peers can be more salient, impactful, and acted upon—whether it is right or wrong—than feedback from teachers.

When students are working together, the teacher needs to be aware that they are not necessarily the main source of feedback as so often happens in the regular whole class situation. So, there is a need to specifically teach students to seek, be open to, evaluate, and be selective in using feedback—from peers, from the Internet, from any source. When the task calls for learning content, facts, and subject matter vocabulary, then it is probably wise for teachers to be more involved in the feedback cycle. But when relating ideas and problem solving, the peers can be much more involved, although teachers may need to check and calibrate the quality and use of feedback within group work. Students need to be taught, and tasks need to be structured, so that feedback is listened to, interpreted, and acted upon.

Learning From a Distance

In distance learning, teach students to give micro-feedback to each other. They can use one of three choices: start/stop/continue to organize the feedback they provide to peers. For example, a student might say, "You should start to use sources when you make a claim because it will make you sound more credible." Or, "You should continue to use adjectives because I think the descriptions are really good and I can get a picture in my mind when I read." Or even, "You might want to stop starting the sentences with the same words. It might be more interesting for your reader to have different starts."

Agency

Agency describes a person's capacity to act and shape one's destiny. It is socially constructed, which is to say that interactions with others influence one's sense of agency. It is dynamic as it ebbs and flows, based in part on past experiences. It is situational, as the task at hand is a factor in whether or not the learner believes that his or her course of action will result in success. For example, the same student can feel a strong sense of agency when it comes to history, but less so with a writing assignment. Bandura (1989) has a far-reaching definition of agency, which includes noting that students can devise ways of adapting flexibly to remarkably diverse environments, they can figure out ways to overcome constraints and barriers, they can redesign and construct environments to their liking, they can create modes of behavior that enable them to realize desired outcomes, and pass on the effective ones to others by social modeling and other experiential modes of influence.

Hitlin and Elder (2007) suggest four overlapping conceptions of agency:

1. Existential agency: The capacity, or free will, for exerting influence on our environments.

2. Programmatic agency: Following rules and routines.

3. Identity agency: What we believe about ourselves and the ways that we wish to be perceived by others.

4. Life-course agency: Actions that we take to affect future outcomes.

But there is a challenge when it comes to issues of agency. As Talsma et al. (2018) note, agency suffers from the "chicken-and-egg" conundrum (p. 137). Which is the causal factor? Is it "I believe, therefore I achieve" or is it "I achieve, therefore I believe?" We may never know the answer to this question, and the answer probably varies and can work both ways. We are confident that agency is important if students are to reap the benefits of collective efficacy. Thus, we take the middle road and focus on both students' achievement and their beliefs. Agency is more likely to occur when students have high expectations of what they can contribute, what the group can teach them, and much confidence in the likelihood of collectively attaining the success criteria.

As we noted in the section on self-efficacy, students need to experience success and thus achieve. And educators can help shape their beliefs, including the ways in which they attribute success, so that agency is developed.

Based on their study of 16,000 sixth through ninth grade classrooms, Ferguson et al. (2015) noted that there were significant differences between students with and without agency. See Figure 3.1 for a visual representation of the differences.

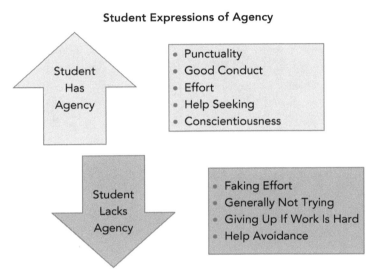

Student Expressions of Agency

Student Has Agency
- Punctuality
- Good Conduct
- Effort
- Help Seeking
- Conscientiousness

Student Lacks Agency
- Faking Effort
- Generally Not Trying
- Giving Up If Work Is Hard
- Help Avoidance

Source: Ferguson et al. (2015).

Figure 3.1

In terms of recommendations for developing student agency, Ferguson et al. (2015) provide several guidelines. Figure 3.2 is organized around seven factors of classroom practice and of group work that can optimize the student agency: care, confer, captivate, consolidate, clarify, challenge, and classroom management.

As you reconsider the scenarios that started this chapter and the ones that focused on self-efficacy, did you notice that the factors related to agency were also featured? Educators carefully consider the interactions they have with students as these interactions can build or damage self-efficacy and agency. Similarly, there is a strong connection to the notion of self-regulation—the ability, confidence, and agency to regulate one's behavior, thinking, and acting. The ultimate expression of these worthwhile notions (agency, self-efficacy, self-regulation, meta-cognition and many more) is when we teach students to become their own teachers—an excellent skill when working with others.

SEVEN FACTORS FOR OPTIMIZING STUDENT AGENCY

Factor	Description	Guidelines for Teaching
Care	Emotional sensitivity and responsiveness	Be attentive and sensitive but avoid a tendency among sensitive teachers to coddle students in ways that may lower standards and undermine agency.
Confer	How welcoming the teacher is to student perspectives	Encourage and respect students' perspectives and honor student voice but do so while remaining focused on instructional goals; avoid extended discussions that have no apparent purpose and thereby fail to model self-discipline and cultivate agency.
Captivate	How captivating classes are	Strive to make lessons stimulating and relevant to the development of agency. If some students seem unresponsive, do not assume too quickly that they are disinterested or disengaged. Some students—and especially those who struggle—purposefully hide their interest and their effort.
Consolidate	Making learning coherent	Regularly summarize lessons to remind students what they have learned and help them encode understanding in memory, even when they seem reticent or disinterested. Consolidation helps to solidify student learning.
Clarity	Clear up confusion	Take regular steps to detect and respond to confusion in class but in ways that share responsibility (and agency) with students for doing the thinking. Strike a balance between keeping hope alive for struggling students, on the one hand, versus pressing them to take responsibility for their own learning, on the other hand.
Clarify	Lucid explanations	Strive to develop clearer explanations—especially for the material that students find most difficult. Also, related to both clarify and captivate, develop lucid explanations of how the skills and knowledge you teach are useful in the exercise of effective agency in real life.
Clarify	Instructive feedback	Give instructive feedback in ways that provide scaffolding for students to solve their own problems; through instructive feedback, you provide the type of support that enables students to develop and express agency by correcting their own work, solving their own problems, and building their own understandings.

(Continued)

(Continued)

Factor	Description	Guidelines for Teaching
Challenge	Require rigor	Press students to think deeply instead of superficially about their lessons; set and enforce learning goals that require students to use reasoning and exercise agency in solving problems. Expect some pushback from students who might prefer a less stressful approach. Try increasing captivation and care in combination with rigor in order to help mitigate the tension and make the experience more enjoyable.
Challenge	Require persistence	Consistently require students to keep trying and searching for ways to succeed even when work is difficult. Emphasize the importance of giving their best efforts to produce their best work as a matter of routine. Be confident that few things could be more important for helping your students to develop agency.
Classroom management	Orderly, respectful, and generally on-task	Strive to achieve respectful, orderly, on-task student behavior in your class by teaching in ways that clarify, captivate, and challenge—in support of agency—instead of merely controlling students through intimidation or coercion.

Source: Ferguson et al. (2015).

Figure 3.2

Now let us consider a different situation and analyze it using the lens of agency.

As the students enter their seventh-grade classroom, their teacher says, "Settle down. Settle down. I want you to read this while I take attendance." The teacher distributes a text about alligators and crocodiles. On the bottom of the text, in large print, it says "Grade 3." Following attendance taking, the teacher asks students if they have ever seen an alligator or a crocodile. Several hands raise and the teacher calls on a student who responds, "Well, on vacation last year, we went to Florida and I saw these crocodiles jump up to catch food. It was really gross, but also cool. We also went to Universal [Studios] but the Harry Potter stuff was just okay."

The teacher responds, "I thought you'd like the Harry Potter exhibit. Did you try the Forbidden Journey ride? I heard it's really cool." The student responded, "No, the lines were too long. We did go on Hagrid's motorcycle ride. The creatures are cool but the ride is kinda boring. My sister liked it a lot but not me."

This conversation continues for a few minutes before the teacher returns to the reading saying, "So, we know that crocodiles and alligators are real. What else did the text tell us?" A student raises his hand and says, "What is a crocodile's favorite drink? Gator-aide, get it?" Another student responds, "Stupid, that would be an alligator's favorite drink, get it?" The first student reacts, saying "I'm not stupid. You are. Stupid, stupid, stupid." The teacher ignores the students and says, "Okay, class, settle down. We need to think about the differences between alligators and crocodiles. Who can tell me one difference so that I can record it on this graphic organizer?"

One student says when one leaves, it says "in a while," while the other says "see you later." The class continued and never really got any better. Can you identify the ways in which student agency was harmed? There are probably more than we can count. But this was a real experience of a well-meaning teacher. He just did not yet understand the impact that his actions had on students. He cared for them but did not teach them. He had low expectations for their success. He tried to honor student voice but lost the focus of the learning. He allowed students to verbally harm each other and thus violated the safety of the learning environment. He did not explain anything and the rigor was seriously compromised. There was no feedback. We could go on, but you get the point.

Learning From a Distance

Before placing students in breakout rooms in virtual classrooms, make sure that they know that they have the responsibility to let you know if they are uncomfortable with any of the interactions they experience. Most systems have a way to anonymously alert the teacher (host) so that you can join the meeting and address the issue. Teaching bystanders their role and holding students accountable for creating a respectful learning environment should be a feature of distance learning. Just like what happened in discussion about crocodiles and alligators, students may not always exhibit kindness to their peers. Randomly visiting rooms and ensuring that students are comfortable with notifying you will reduce this and allow you to maintain a productive learning environment online.

Resilience

Students must be able to face and embrace challenge and further understand that failure is potentially an opportunity to learn. However, students who are less resilient avoid challenge and thus are prevented from learning from mistakes. Life experiences play an important role, and trauma, food insecurity, racism, and other significant stressors impact a student's resilience. Having said that, Vogel and Schwabe (2016) believe that "stressful events do not necessarily lead to a stress response, but that the individual appraisal of the situation and the available coping strategies determine whether a situation results in the activation of stress systems or not" (p. 7). Resilience, like all of these other constructs presented in this chapter, is influenced by personality and dispositions, too, such as optimism and hopefulness. It also needs to be applied in the right circumstance, at the right time—which is why many generic programs to develop resilience (grit or growth mindset) fail whereas those developed in the context of the situation are more successful. And, like the other constructs presented in this chapter, the adults in the lives of children and youth can impact resilience.

Some have portrayed resilience as grit, which has become quite popular; and there are many similar constructs: willpower, tenacity, determination, growth mindset, and persistence. We prefer to distinguish between two major aspects of grit: perseverance of effort (some students will stick with a problem or challenge, whereas others give up), and conscientiousness (some students will stay with a subject and be less keen to change goals or interests). The first is when students welcome appropriately challenging goals, the second when students are willing to invest many hours on a task. Both seem important, but perhaps they should not be added together as they are different and can lead to different teaching interventions and task demands for each (see Credé et al., 2017; Ris, 2015).

The American Psychological Association has identified ten actions that parents and educators can take to develop resilience (perseverance and conscientiousness) in young people. As noted in Figure 3.3, these recommendations require that teachers carefully consider the interactions they have with students and the ways in which learning environments are structured.

Edgar Torres uses literature to provoke conversations with his second-grade students that develop their "I" skills, including resilience. As he says, "I think resilience is an important skill for students to develop, not

1. **Make connections**

   Teach your child how to make friends, including the skill of empathy, or feeling another's pain. Encourage your child to be a friend in order to get friends. Build a strong family network to support your child through his or her inevitable disappointments and hurts. At school, watch to make sure that one child is not being isolated. Connecting with people provides social support and strengthens resilience. Some find comfort in connecting with a higher power, whether through organized religion or privately and you may wish to introduce your child to your own traditions of worship.

2. **Help your child by having him or her help others**

   Children who may feel helpless can be empowered by helping others. Engage your child in age-appropriate volunteer work or ask for assistance yourself with some task that he or she can master. At school, brainstorm with children about ways they can help others.

3. **Maintain a daily routine**

   Sticking to a routine can be comforting to children, especially younger children who crave structure in their lives. Encourage your child to develop his or her own routines.

4. **Take a break**

   While it is important to stick to routines, endlessly worrying can be counter-productive. Teach your child how to focus on something besides what's worrying him. Be aware of what your child is exposed to that can be troubling, whether it be news, the Internet, or overheard conversations, and make sure your child takes a break from those things if they trouble her. Although schools are being held accountable for performance on standardized tests, build in unstructured time during the school day to allow children to be creative.

5. **Teach your child self-care**

   Make yourself a good example, and teach your child the importance of making time to eat properly, exercise, and rest. Make sure your child has time to have fun, and make sure that your child hasn't scheduled every moment of his or her life with no "down time" to relax. Caring for oneself and even having fun will help your child stay balanced and better deal with stressful times.

6. **Move toward your goals**

   Teach your child to set reasonable goals and then to move toward them one step at a time. Moving toward that goal—even if it's a tiny step—and receiving praise for doing so will focus your child on what he or she has accomplished rather than on what hasn't been accomplished and can help build the resilience to move forward in the face of challenges. At school, break down large assignments into small, achievable goals for younger children, and for older children, acknowledge accomplishments on the way to larger goals.

(Continued)

(Continued)

7. **Nurture a positive self-view**

   Help your child remember ways that he or she has successfully handled hardships in the past and then help him understand that these past challenges help him build the strength to handle future challenges. Help your child learn to trust himself to solve problems and make appropriate decisions. Teach your child to see the humor in life and the ability to laugh at oneself. At school, help children see how their individual accomplishments contribute to the well-being of the class as a whole.

8. **Keep things in perspective and maintain a hopeful outlook**

   Even when your child is facing very painful events, help him look at the situation in a broader context and keep a long-term perspective. Although your child may be too young to consider a long-term look on his own, help him or her see that there is a future beyond the current situation and that the future can be good. An optimistic and positive outlook enables your child to see the good things in life and keep going even in the hardest times. In school, use history to show that life moves on after bad events.

9. **Look for opportunities for self-discovery**

   Tough times are often the times when children learn the most about themselves. Help your child take a look at how whatever he is facing can teach him "what he is made of." At school, consider leading discussions of what each student has learned after facing down a tough situation.

10. **Accept that change is part of living**

    Change often can be scary for children and teens. Help your child see that change is part of life and new goals can replace goals that have become unattainable. In school, point out how students have changed as they moved up in grade levels and discuss how that change has had an impact on the students.

Source: https://www.apa.org/helpcenter/resilience

Figure 3.3

only for their collaboration with others at school, but in life. But I want my students to know that there are times when we should be resilient and times when we need to resist or protest. I like to use children's literature to have these conversations. For example, we read *Harvesting Hope* (Krull, 2003) about the life of Cesar Chavez and his decision not to put up with the working conditions for people working on farms. We talked about rights and when rights are violated, people have other options to just accept the way things are. Other times, we read books that allow for us to talk about resilience in a healthy way."

Mr. Torres introduced the book *I Want It* (Crary, 1982), which introduces two characters who both want to play with the same truck. Readers get to choose what happens to Amy and Megan and if they don't like their choice, they can make a different choice and see what happens. It's rather like the "choose your own adventure" stories from years ago. But this book focuses on being resilient and learning to problem solve and compromise. The students in Mr. Torres's class had a conversation about their choices and the impact that each choice had on the characters. As Miguel said, "I think that Amy should just get a different toy. They have lots of toys in the room." Mr. Torres responded, "That's one option, right? But what if that made Amy feel bad? Is that the only option these two people have?"

The conversation continued with students voicing ideas and opinions. At one point, Ana Maria said, "Next time, when I want the same thing as Karla, I will say we can share. And if she doesn't want to, I know that I can have a turn later and it's not a problem. But I think we can learn to share better." Importantly, these conversations are not one-and-done. Students in Mr. Torres's class are learning to read and write using literature that also allows them to discuss "I" skills that will serve them well. The writing prompt for the day they read *I Want It* invited students to consider the perspective of Megan.

The prompt read:

> *After reading "I Want It," write a summary in which you explain*
> *Megan's actions and feelings based on the solution you chose.*
> *Support your response with evidence from the text.*

The students are developing their literacy prowess, specifically being taught how to summarize information. But the added benefit is that Mr. Torres gets a glimpse into the thinking process of his students and comes to understand the types of experiences they need to have to continue to develop their skills, including resilience.

Communication Skills

There are a range of communication skills that students need to be successful in school and in life. Many of these communication skills develop as students have chances to interact with other people. Students need the outward skills of communication (e.g., eye contact, nonverbal, gestural, and body language skills) as well as active listening skills. These include being attentive, asking related questions, requesting clarification, noticing the emotions of others, and being able to summarize and restate. In addition, effective communicators are able to clearly explain, provide evidence, gain and yield the floor, and move the group forward in its task.

In general, content standards developed by many national governments include communication skills. These are typically part of the English language arts or reading expectations, but they extend across the curriculum and grades. Unfortunately, since these standards are often not tested, they are neglected. This is problematic because communication skills are foundational to collective efficacy as well as success later in life.

Mattie Johnson, a third-grade teacher, knows the value of communication skills. As she says, "Developing strong communication skills is the foundation for everything else we do. I want my students to learn from each other and me and that requires communication." One of the standards for her grade level requires that students "Explain their own ideas and understanding in light of the discussion." As a habit, Ms. Johnson engages her students in classroom discussions. During the discussion she asks students to summarize what another student has said and then explain their own ideas. As she says, "I want the conversations and discussions in my classroom to build. I want students to recognize the thinking of their peers and note where they agree and disagree. At the start of the year, we used the sentence frames 'I agree with . . . because . . .' or 'I respectfully disagree with. . . . because . . .' to provide students practice with this type of interaction. As they developed their skills in communicating, we dropped the frames."

Ms. Johnson uses the information found in Figure 3.4 to help guide her students' communication skills. Students have a copy of this at their desks and there is a large poster version hanging on a classroom wall. During a social studies discussion about cost and benefit, the students read a short article about the worldwide supply of milk. During their discussion, the students drew on their experiences with the guidelines rather than having their teacher mediate the conversation. In many classrooms, one student

ACTIVE LISTENING AND SPEAKING GUIDELINES

What to Do	Why Do It	How to Do It	Examples of What to Say
Encourage	To convey interest in what the speaker is discussing. To keep the person talking.	Nod, smile, and use other facial expressions. Don't agree or disagree. Use noncommittal words with positive tone of voice.	"I see . . ." "uh-uh" "Yes . . ." "That's really interesting . . ."
Restate or Clarify	To show that you are listening and understand. To check your perception of the speaker's message.	Restate the basic ideas, emphasizing the facts. Clarify points. Don't fake listen!	"If I understand, your idea is . . ." "I see what you mean" "In other words, this is . . ." "What did you mean when you said . . .?"
Reflect or Paraphrase	To show the speaker that what they are saying is being heard. To show you understand their feelings.	Restate the other's basic feelings. Respond to the other's main ideas.	"You feel that . . ." "You must feel angry that . . ." "I think you're very happy that . . ."
Summarize	To pull important ideas, facts, etc. together. To establish a basis for further discussion. To review progress.	Restate, reflect, and summarize major ideas and feelings.	"So would you say the key ideas are . . .?" "If I understand you, you're saying that . . ." "Based on your presentation would it be accurate to say that . . .?"

Figure 3.4

speaks and then the teacher assumes responsibility, either adding a comment or directing attention to the next student speaker. After the second student speaks, the teacher re-assumes responsibility, commenting or directing attention to the next speaker. This continues, with the entire conversation being mediated by the teacher. This is likely to develop some individual communication skills for students, but they will be hard pressed to engage in a fruitful conversation with a small group of peers if their teacher always mediates their interactions.

Ms. Johnson refrains from interjecting and only does so when the conversation gets stuck, when there is factual information that needs to be clarified, or when two students are simply going back and forth without adding others to the conversation. Most of the time, she does not need to mediate the discussion as her students have a great deal of experience with whole class and small group discussions. As Ms. Johnson notes, "You don't get good at something you don't do. I devote a lot of time for students to practice their communication skills. I observe so that I can provide feedback and additional instruction when I notice that there is unfinished learning."

During their conversation about cost and benefit, the students noted that the price was not just the cost, which seemed to be an ah-ha moment for many of them. Part of their discussion included the following discussion:

Jamie:	The price is how much they make you pay, right?
Paul:	Yes, it's the cost and the amount of money they want to make for profit.
Karina:	That's really interesting. Explain it again.
Paul:	Okay, so this is what I think it means. There is a price for the milk, right? It's how much money you have to pay for it. But that price is more than how much it cost to get the milk.
Angela:	I think you are saying that the price and the cost can be different, right?
Karina:	That's what I think now, too. There is the cost to get the product, like milk. But they have to sell it for more or they don't have a profit.
Paul:	See? That's the key idea. There is a difference between cost and price. But I am not sure how much the profit is.

Their conversation continued as they explored cost and eventually turned to benefit. Ms. Johnson monitored the conversation, taking notes as her students interacted. She tracked which students spoke and what they had to say so that she could provide feedback and instruction following the discussion.

High school career and technical education teacher Peter Wotring focuses on the types of communication skills necessary in the world of work. He provides his students with the communication skills and tips developed by Businessphrases.net. As part of his class, students watch video clips of various interactions and analyze the moves of each of the speakers and listeners using the skills sheet (Figure 3.5). For example, the students were asked to watch a video from a group of students the previous year. Mr. Wotring asked his students to focus on:

- body language
- eye contact
- summarizing
- paraphrasing
- responding

As he said, "I think that there is a lot to learn from observing others. Let's see how these students did with our five focus areas for this month. Make sure you take notes so that you can reference specific behaviors of speakers when you share your thinking." Following the video, students were asked to share with a partner. Mr. Wotring said, "Discuss each of the five we are focused on this month. See if you can reach consensus and note where you disagree."

The students spent the next eight minutes discussing their ideas. Omar said, "I think that their body language was all really good. They were open and relaxed. They nodded and showed that they were interested."

His partner Alisa agreed, adding, "I especially like how they track the speaker with their body language. It is obvious who they are listening to. I think that the problem really was paraphrasing. I didn't really hear that, did you?"

Omar responded, "Not really. But I don't think it hurt their conversation. They didn't paraphrase but the discussion seemed really good and they got some good information out on the table. I think we should ask Mr. Wotring if paraphrasing is always required. I think it slows things down sometimes and that there are good times to use it but not always."

COMMUNICATION SKILLS AND TIPS

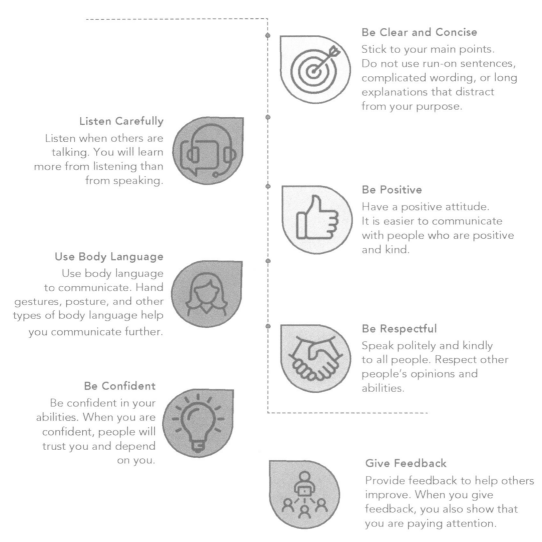

Be Clear and Concise
Stick to your main points. Do not use run-on sentences, complicated wording, or long explanations that distract from your purpose.

Listen Carefully
Listen when others are talking. You will learn more from listening than from speaking.

Be Positive
Have a positive attitude. It is easier to communicate with people who are positive and kind.

Use Body Language
Use body language to communicate. Hand gestures, posture, and other types of body language help you communicate further.

Be Respectful
Speak politely and kindly to all people. Respect other people's opinions and abilities.

Be Confident
Be confident in your abilities. When you are confident, people will trust you and depend on you.

Give Feedback
Provide feedback to help others improve. When you give feedback, you also show that you are paying attention.

Adapted from: www.businessphrases.net/examples-good-communication-skills and images from iStock.com/fonikum

Figure 3.5

Alisa responded, "That's really interesting. In our groups, we always make sure that someone paraphrases. But I see how it can slow down the conversation, especially when everyone is already agreeing."

As the timer rang, Mr. Wotring invited each partnership to square up with another partner, forming a group of four. "As you discuss, see where you agree and where you disagree. I'd like each group to have a talking point when we come back together in eight minutes. Then we'll see what we learned from these students and how we can improve our communication skills."

Learning From a Distance

Communication skills are critical, irrespective of the format of schooling. A critical component of distance learning is student-to-student interaction. Teachers need to teach these communication skills and provide students opportunities to practice these skills, making mistakes and receiving feedback so that they can improve. The think-pair-square process is a useful way to provide students interaction opportunities. In the main room, students are provided time to read, view, or listen and think. Then they are moved into breakout rooms with two people per room. After a pre-determined amount of time, the rooms are combined so that they are now four students in each room. This allows for the same experience described in Mr. Wotring's class.

Now, we will focus on a seemingly minuscule aspect of communication: taking turns while interacting. Turn-taking in a group is very important. It turns out that many aspects of turn-taking, such as timing, are remarkably stable across languages and cultures. It involves anticipating the other person's pauses, avoiding overlap, minimizing silences between turns, sometimes ignoring the other and merely waiting to reenter the conversation, and sometimes flowing from the other's turn. The flow is higher when the individual is listening and making predictions about when the speaker will end and the next speech utterances, allowing the listener to decide when to speak and what to say next (Holler et al., 2016). The skills of turn-taking begin developing between two to five months of age (Dominguez et al., 2016) yet many students still need to be taught the skills of turn-taking, if working with others is to be of value.

The chart shown in Figure 3.6 shows a classroom rubric that students use to guide their turn-taking in partner conversations.

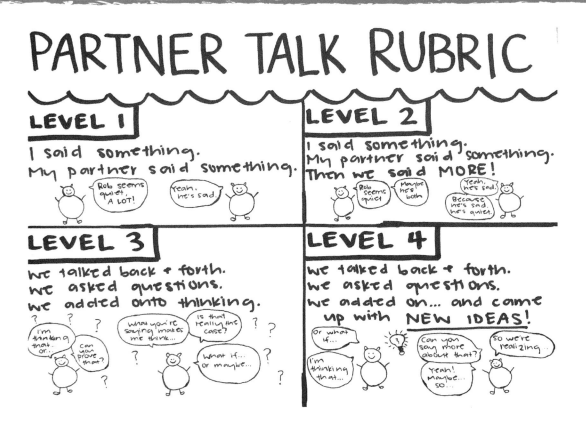

Figure 3.6

It is well worth modeling turn taking by the teacher. This begins by being aware of our dominant role in the discourse of whole classes. In many classes, teachers focus more on what they are teaching and what their students are meant to be learning and pay less attention to what it means to be a student listening into classroom discourse and involving students in the give and take of the dialogue in classes. Teachers are often surprised when we show our data that on average teachers talk more than 80 percent of the time, the high levels of recitation, the limited student discussion time, and how their "wait time" can usually be measured in milliseconds and the typical student response is less than three words (see Alexander, 2020). As many have shown, the dominant discourse is teacher's initiation, a response usually from one student, and teacher feedback, and so this pattern is continued (Kyriacou & Issitt, 2008).

When the teacher is interacting with students, they often not only ask questions with pre-scripted answers and attribute speaking turns to students but they also control the theme and flow of the discussion—often directly opposite to what happens in conversation between students (and indeed in most social interactions). Mimicking what teachers do when they teach is not what is desired in student groups, as it implies a dominant, knowledgeable single individual in control. Instead, more soft transitions, pausing, lacing between ideas, supportive interruptions, sharing, and critiquing of ideas are needed.

Nystrand and Gamoran (1997) made the strong claim: the bottom line for learning is the extent to which instruction requires students to think, not just report someone else's thinking. Dialogue means that knowing is not only transmitted but negotiated. Alexander (2020) outlines eight justifications for enabling students to engage in dialogue:

1. Talk for thinking
2. Talk for learning
3. Talk for mastery
4. Talk for communication
5. Talk for relating
6. Talk for acculturation
7. Talk for democratic engagement
8. Talk for teaching

And talk is core to the dialogue of learning when it is collective (shared among students and with the teacher), supportive (when students feel they can express ideas freely), reciprocal (when they consider alternative viewpoints), deliberative (leading to resolving different points of view), and purposeful (is structured toward learning intentions and success criteria).

Moving from the teacher to student to teacher—the usual talking pattern—to engaging students in talking with each other builds core skills for working in teams: asking questions about what they do not know and building off of each other in their thinking and understanding.

In regular conversation between children, generally only one person speaks at a time, overlaps between speakers are short, and there are no gaps when the speaker changes. There is a "togetherness" in the conversational relationship, and more speaking for the "we" who are the participants. Students more than teachers engage in highly desirable "uptake" dialogue when the next speaker incorporates answers or dialogue from the previous speaker and does not end in another question (Nystrand et al., 2003). When questions are asked, they tend to not presume the speaker has prespecified an answer, such as requests for information as well as open-ended questions with indeterminate answers. Turn-taking is the essence of successful group interactions.

There are a number of ways that teachers can help students develop their turn-taking skills. For example, Brad Jacobson provides each of his second-grade students with three gaming chips. As they contribute to their group, they place a chip in a basket in the middle of their table. When they have run out of chips, they have to listen and can't yet add anything to the group. When everyone has exhausted all of their chips, students can add information to the group. As Mr. Jacobson says, "It's kinda artificial and I just use this to teach them that no one should talk the entire time. I want them to see that there should be some turn-taking. It doesn't control for how long someone talks, just that everyone gets a number of turns."

In Andrea Bianchi's middle school history class, each group is provided with a visual clue that indicates the person who should be speaking. As they take turns, students pass the "talking stick" to a peer and that person has a chance to share. As Ms. Bianchi notes, "I think that this helps students focus on the speaker, but I want the conversations to become more natural, with give-and-take, over time. I use the talking stick to focus on taking turns and learning to listen to others, but there are times when I just have students talk to see if they are generalizing any of the turn-taking skills."

One of the thoughts for teachers when they are engaged in turn-taking is to note who takes the third turn. After the teacher turn, then the student turn, who goes next? The answer should be "not always the teacher."

Sometimes, teachers use timers to teach students how long each turn should last. That can be an effective way for the listener to learn wait time and for the speaker to judge how long each contribution should last. Another way to force the turn-taking is to assign each student a

SELF-ASSESSMENT OF GROUP PARTICIPATION

Statement	Always	Sometimes	Seldom
I contributed ideas to the group.			
I listened to and respected the members of the group.			
I took turns as group members shared.			
I came to the group prepared to work.			
I cooperated with my group members.			
I did my fair share of the work for this project.			

Figure 3.7

letter or position and then identify which person should be talking in the group. For example, kindergarten teacher Amelia Brodeur regularly stops her read alouds and says, "Person A, it's your turn to share with person B." Later, she will stop again and say, "Person B, it's your turn to share with person A." Each of these teachers has provided students with practice in turn-taking so that they know what it feels like. But these instructional tools eventually need to be removed and students need to learn how to interact with group members, naturally engaging in turn-taking. Reflection tools, such as the one in Figure 3.7, can help students think about their contributions to the group and to identify areas in which they still need work.

Learning From a Distance

Self-assessment tools like the one in Figure 3.7 can be used as exit polls at the end of synchronous learning sessions. In addition, students can be provided opportunities in their asynchronous sessions to self-assess and write a reflection about their contributions to their group. This information should be used to design additional learning experiences for students so that their skills continue to grow such that collective efficacy is enhanced.

THE PAIDEIA METHOD

The Paideia method was developed by Adler (1998) and implemented by Roberts and Billings (1999). It has three components: Didactic instruction, Socratic seminars, and coached projects with the suggestion of about one-third of each across a series of lessons. The didactic stage provides an opportunity for students to gain domain and strategic knowledge for them to participate in the seminars from informed positions. The key to Socratic questioning is the provision of a thought-provoking, open-ended question based on rich and challenging texts that lead to the development of critical ideas (texts includes much more than written sources, such as music, a painting, a car manual). The seminar aims to promote inquiry and allows ideas to be probed, grappled with, and tested. The open question and format are not about coming to the "right answer" but to help students focus on the processes of thinking and examine their own and others' thinking and arguments.

The coached project is a production or performance that demonstrates mastery of a subject to an audience outside the classroom. It has a focus on rigorous, relevant, and quality work measured against various criteria of success. Given its audience is not just the teacher, the focus of assessment changes, and students are often more willing to reach for higher standards. "We believe, however, that the desire to construct a tangible product of the highest quality is a powerful motivator for students, especially when that product has both intrinsic value for the students and value to an authentic external audience. Only when they sense the relevance and authenticity of classroom work will most students commit to the very real labor of learning" (Roberts & Trainor, 2004, p. 515).

John was part of the team evaluating the implementation of Paideia (Hattie et al., 1998), and he was so impressed he decided to try it himself. He taught his two-hour class on Messick's concept of validity (in a course on Test Development), and the students answered all the questions, worked together to solve problems, and wrote copious notes. Then to the next class and Socratic seminar. John grouped the students in a circle, worked hard to devise and then ask an "open" question, and perhaps the hardest skill was then to shut up. While he listened, he drew a social network diagram of who spoke to whom. The purpose was not the sociogram but to show students that it was up to them. The students continually looked to John for input and prompts—they did not want to talk aloud to each other—but when they did, they asked some silly questions and gave each other some wrong answers. The seminar was an eye opener to his impact. Despite the way John "controlled" and believed he was so good (as did the students in their evaluations), it was via this experience teaching with Paideia that forever changed his lecturing methods.

The Paideia method has a balance of teacher-led teaching, student-led teaching, openness to hearing student thinking and errors, constructing and deconstructing ideas, and ensuring students work together in the coached project (see Billings & Fitzgerald, 2002; Haroutunian-Gordon, 1998; Orellana, 2008; Pihlgren, 2008; Robinson, 2006; Robinson & Lai, 2006). Davies and Sinclair (2014) showed that the Paideia method led to more complex, deeper thinking compared to regular teaching on the same topics. This was particularly because of the nature of interactions between students and between students and the teacher. These interactions involved students seeking evidence and justifications for their thoughts, "agreeing with each other and then expanding with further information; students disagreeing with each other and then expanding on why they disagreed with each other; students responding back to the student who had disagreed with them and explaining themselves further and students asking another student a question" (p. 39). They also noted that students in their low- compared to high-socio-economic schools needed longer teacher didactic teaching and teaching skills of dialogue as opposed to recitation for the fruits to pay off in the Socratic and coached project phases. This is similar to the claims by Wilkinson and Son (2010) about implementing their Quality Talk processes:

- Use ground rules to establish the norms of productive talk.
- Use authentic questions and follow-up, uptake questions to give students opportunities to engage in productive talk.
- Use informal assessment strategies during discussions, listening for evidence of the elements of talk that indicate higher level thinking.

Paolo Freire (1996) who developed a pedagogy of liberation claims about the power and misuse of power of teaching sums up this chapter nicely: "Authentic help means that all who are involved help each other mutually, growing together in the common effort to understand the reality, which they seek to transform. Only through such praxis—in which those who help and those who are being helped, help each other simultaneously—can the act of helping become free from the distortion in which the helper dominates the helped."

In this chapter, we have profiled a number of skills that students need to develop, especially if we are to capitalize on the power of collective student efficacy. To learn with others, and to develop the belief in the power of the collective, students must develop the "I" skills described above. But collective student efficacy is more than putting students together in a group and hoping for the best. Pushing the desks together does not automatically ensure that collective efficacy is realized. In addition to the "I" skills, students need to develop a set of "we" skills.

CHAPTER 4

DEVELOPING THE "WE" SKILLS

In this chapter we will explore the "We" skills necessary for students to be successful as they work and learn with their peers. Of course, the "I" and "We" sets of skills are not isolated and independent. Rather, both are complementary and necessary to be successful in collective experiences. Collective efficacy is more than adding up the individual efficacy of each member of a group. There is a synergy that happens when group members believe that they can make a difference, when they mobilize their individual and collective skills, and when they identify evidence that their collective efforts are effective.

Developing Shared Beliefs

Collective efficacy rests on a set of beliefs, namely the belief that the group has the combined ability to be successful. Or as Bandura defined it, collective efficacy is "a group's shared belief in its conjoint capability to organize and execute the courses of action required to produce given levels of attainment" (1997, p. 477). This is one of the "we" skills that is hard to teach. It develops over time and with experience. As students experience groups that "produce"—and by that we mean they complete assigned tasks and learn from those tasks—individual members of the group come to believe that groups can be an effective and efficient way to work and learn. We focus on the types of tasks that are effective in producing these beliefs in Chapter 5. In this chapter, we focus on helping students develop positive and productive beliefs about groups.

It turns out that this is fairly hard to do. A belief is something that we consider a fact or have confidence that it is correct. Beliefs develop based on experiences and what other people tell us. As Shermer (2011) notes, more often we form our beliefs first and then look for evidence in support of them afterward. Shermer explains that this is due, in a large part, to the way our brains work. He notes two aspects, in particular: We look for patterns, and we love to assign causal relationships. Together, these two aspects result in a "belief engine" as our brains are always seeking to find meaning from the information that pours into it. Once a belief is formed, our brains rationalize the belief with explanations, ignoring information that is not consistent with the belief. So, what does this have to do with collective student efficacy? To our thinking, a lot.

As educators, we have to work to ensure that students believe that their group work will be useful, effective, and fun, and that they will be successful and can learn a lot. It starts with the teacher's attitudes toward the collaborative tasks. When introducing tasks that require student-to-student interaction and collaboration, the teacher should be enthusiastic and positive. Teachers should not minimize the value of the task. We once observed a teacher say, "We have a little job to do today. It's not too hard so don't really worry about it. It will get done faster if you work in groups. It's just practice and I'm not going to grade it."

That all may be true, but imagine the beliefs that are being reinforced as the task is explained. There are several problematic aspects of this explanation, including the fact that there is nothing wrong with practice and we don't assign group tasks simply to make things go faster. But our point here is to note that teachers' enthusiasm, especially when they are credible with their students, builds the belief system that is so important for collective efficacy to be developed.

It is also important to note that early collaborative experiences should provide students with opportunities to be successful. For example, if you are introducing a new collaborative reading procedure, it is wise to reduce the difficulty of the text so that students can focus on the process. As an example, the students in Milton Hage's middle school science class were learning about potential and kinetic energy. They had watched a video clip that had explained these concepts. Mr. Hage had several readings for students and selected the one that was the least complex to start. He introduced a new collaborative procedure called

PROCEDURES FOR TEXT RENDERING

- Meet in groups and appoint a scribe.

- **Round 1:** Each person shares a significant sentence.

- **Round 2**: Each person shares a significant phrase (scribe records).

- **Round 3**: Each person shares a significant word (scribe records).

- The group discusses what they heard and what it says about the document.

- The group shares the words that emerged and any new insights about the document.

- The group debriefs the text rendering process.

Figure 4.1

Text Rendering (see Figure 4.1) which was new to his students. He said, "I recently learned a new collaborative reading process. The science teachers have all been using this when we read things together and I really like it. I wanted to share it with you because I think it really helps identify important information in a text. Remember that we are focused on potential and kinetic energy, and the article that we're going to read is really cool. It is about roller coasters! We will read more about these forms of energy this week, but we start with a ride. And, as we will learn, there is potential and kinetic energy all around us. We will become experts on this topic and we will see energy everywhere we look. So, here's how Text Rendering works."

He explained the procedure and his students got to work, reading the text, and identifying sentences, phrases, and words that they might like to share with their group members. He visited groups to check in with them, adding comments and asking questions as he interacted with students. His enthusiasm and his plan for students to be successful while learning the required content helped to reinforce students' beliefs about their groups.

Learning From a Distance

Text rendering is one of the collaborative tasks that works very well in distance learning. Students read the text in advance or while they are in the main room. Their task at that time is to identify a sentence, phrase, and word that they found significant. Once they have finished the reading, they move into breakout groups to render the text, recording their sentences, phrases, and words in a Google doc that allows each member of the group, as well as the teacher, to monitor their progress. Once all of the ideas are out on the virtual table, they discuss what they heard. Students will ask each other about their selections and what different parts of the text mean. In doing so, they deepen their understanding of the text and attribute success to their group.

As we will discuss in Chapter 6 on Learning Intentions and Success criteria, teachers have to ensure that the success criteria that appropriately stretch the group are optimal and then make sure there is appropriate scaffolding, feedback, resources, and confidence in the group to attain these criteria.

Unfortunately, sometimes beliefs are already set and teachers have to help students modify those beliefs. We have lost count of the number of people who have told us about experiences with group work gone bad. Claims like, "But only one person in the group did any work," and usually it is the person telling us the story. The beliefs that have developed and have been reinforced are anti-group and anti-collective efficacy. This person sees no value from working with others and instead sees the group tasks as perfunctory.

When students have negative beliefs about group tasks, they are not likely to benefit from the power of collective efficacy. To change those beliefs, students need to be confronted with evidence to the contrary. Yes, as Shermer (2011) noted, information not consistent with existing beliefs is often ignored. But beliefs can change with some persistence and a little peer support.

Collective Student Efficacy in Action

This is exactly what happened in Jessica Machado's ninth grade English class. The students came from a number of different middle schools and many had developed positive beliefs about peer-mediated learning. In fact, some of them had great experiences with group learning and Brianna even asked, at the start of the year, "Ms. Machado, do we do group work in your class? Last year, when I transferred to Thompson Middle school, my grades went way up because I learned more with other kids. Before, we had to do all of the work alone and I did not always understand it. At Thompson, we had to figure out things together and my groups were really good at it so I learned more."

But Ms. Machado's classes were not filled with students like Brianna who had extensive positive experiences with the power of collective student efficacy. Anthony, for example, told his teacher that he hated group work because it made him feel stupid. He continued, saying, "All the other kids already know what the poem or book is about. I don't get it and they laugh. I'm not good at English. I got an F last year because I never understood what we were reading."

Ms. Machado planned a series of short collaborative tasks for students, carefully placing students in groups to ensure that there would be models who knew how to interact and support the learning of others. She started with a reversible poem called "Pretty Ugly" by Abdullah Shoaib. Read in one direction, it's very sad but read in the other direction, it's empowering. Ms. Machado started by asking students to read the poem. She did not tell them it was reversible. The groups discussed their reactions to the person and what the person might have experienced to make him or her write such a sad poem. As Ms. Machado said, "There are many right answers to these questions. Just make sure that you reference lines from the poem as evidence when you share your ideas."

Ms. Machado joined Anthony's group first knowing that she needed to highlight any evidence that the group was effective if she was going to confront his beliefs. When Lamar said, "I think someone musta told her that she was a terrible person lots of times. You don't say that about yourself unless you hear it a lot from other people. Like maybe her mom told her she was terrible since she was a baby or something'."

Anthony responded, "I was thinking the same thing. My mom never told me I was terrible or anything, but if she did, I would probably start to think that about myself too. But it also says that the person still deserves love, so he or she hasn't given up totally yet." At that point, Ms. Machado smiled at Anthony and wrote a note on a piece of paper, slipping it to him as she walked away. The note simply said, "You contributed to the group and it helped them think about the meaning of the poem. And did you learn something from others?"

When she was satisfied with their understanding of the poem in the top-down direction, she asked them to read it, bottom up this time. Anthony couldn't help himself and turned to his group, saying "That just blew my mind. Both things are going on for this person at the same time." At the end of the lesson, Ms. Machado provided students with a template for writing reversible poems and invited students to work on their own poems that they could share with others. Anthony raised his hand and asked if they could write a draft and have time with the group to share before they were due to her. Smiling again, Ms. Machado agreed that it would be a good idea to draft poems and get audience reactions before they were due for a grade.

This one day did not radically change Anthony's beliefs about groups, but it was a start. There were days when the group tasks did not work for him and there were days when they really worked. But he started collecting more positive examples and interactions, slowly changing his belief, and coming to realize that he could learn from others and that there were groups that were effective and efficient in ensuring learning. Anthony developed increased social sensitivity, which Brianna and others already had. And that social sensitivity served him well as he began to harness the power of collective student efficacy.

Social Sensitivity

Of all the "I" and "We" skills required for collective student efficacy, the next two are dominant if groups are to be successful:

1. The individuals' capability to be socially sensitive to others
2. The collective potency of the group

We will focus on the first one in this section. Being socially sensitive means that students understand the perspective of others. When they do so, the potential for collective intelligence increases. Thomas Malone coined the term "collective intelligence" and it is now widely used to describe the shared or group intelligence that develops from the collaboration and collective efforts of groups of individuals.

There are three actions or aspects of groups that are highly correlated with collective intelligence (Woolley et al., 2015), including:

1. The amount of turn-taking
2. The group's average levels of social sensitivity
3. The group's proportion of females

We have already discussed turn taking in the section on communication (Chapter 3). Social sensitivity is equally important. Rowe (2019) confirmed that social sensitivity and conversational turn-taking played a significant and critical role in collective intelligence. Rowe also identified factors that were not very important in the development of collective intelligence. These included the

- maximum ability of the group, meaning having really high performing individuals did not result in greater collective intelligence,
- minimum ability of the group, meaning having relatively lower performing individuals did not result in less collective intelligence,
- personality factors of openness to experience, extraversion, neuroticism, agreeableness,
- gender combination of the group, and
- proportion of friends within the group.

So, we know some attributes that do not matter so much, and these are in stark contrast to the importance of social sensitivity. In sum, collective intelligence develops when members of the group exhibit social sensitivity. Social sensitivity is the student's ability to stand in other's shoes—to perceive, understand, and respect the feelings and viewpoints of others. It involves the ability to acknowledge mistakes, accept others as they are, decode what others are thinking and feeling, problem solve about what is happening in the group to move it forward, empathize with others and with the group's moods and feelings, and listen and demonstrate they have listened to others in the group (Bender et al., 2012). Social sensitivity is especially important when dealing with more complex than simple tasks, as then there are many more opportunities for errors, a higher need to search for new information, more chance of faulty decision-making, and greater need to attend to the views of others.

Thankfully, social sensitivity can be taught, nurtured, and developed. In part, this requires that teachers focus on developing students' empathy. Again, there are a wide range of books that provide students opportunities to see how others are, or are not, empathetic. Some of the titles useful in exploring empathy include:

- *Last Stop on Market Street* by Matt de la Peña
- *Those Shoes* by Maribeth Boelts
- *Most People* by Michael Leannah
- *Wonder* by R. J. Palacio
- *The Perks of Being a Wallflower* by Stephen Chbosky
- *No Longer at Ease* by Chinua Achebe

Borba (2018) believes that effective empathy education requires adherence to seven core principles guided by strong, empathetic school leaders.

1. **Ongoing:** Educating for empathy is not a one-time lesson, but a continual focus.

2. **Woven-In:** Empathy competencies are integrated into content and interactions, not tacked on.

3. **Meaningful:** Instruction is authentic, touches the heart and mind, and stretches "me" to "we."

4. **Internalized:** The goal is for students to adopt empathy competencies as lifelong habits.

5. **Student-Centered:** Students' needs, not curriculum, drive the lessons and experiences.

6. **Respectful Relationships:** Empathy breeds in a culture of respect and caring.

7. **Empathic Leadership:** Empathy is modeled, expected, and core to a principal's vision, purpose, style, and interactions. (p. 28)

Empathy is a worthwhile goal, in and of itself. But it also facilitates social sensitivity, which builds collective intelligence, and that fuels collective student efficacy. There are all important ideas that need to be implemented if students are going to benefit from the collaborative learning structures teachers put in place.

Collective Student Efficacy in Action

A key part of empathy is the students' skills in perspective taking. Again, literature can help, but only when different and diverse perspectives are presented and analyzed. Fourth grade teacher Hiroko Tanaka introduced perspective with the book *Voices in the Park* (Browne, 2001). This book addresses the themes of alienation and friendships, with different characters telling the same story from their own perspectives. Ms. Tanaka notes, "I want my students to develop an understanding that the same experience can be interpreted from different perspectives. Of course, there are inaccurate perspectives but there are often many valid perspectives. We read a lot of books that focus on perspective taking and then I ask my students to consider the perspectives of the other members of the group, referring back to some of the books we have discussed in class."

Ms. Tanaka also uses a structured writing prompt that requires students assume different roles, and thus perspectives, as they construct their responses. The RAFT prompt (Santa & Havens, 1995) focuses on the role, audience, format, and topic (see Figure 4.2). Teachers can change the role and audience regularly so that students get practice with different perspectives, even from the same text. For example, after reading and discussing the book *Yeh-Shen: A Cinderella Story from China* (Louie, 1996) as part of their exploration of Cinderella stories from around the world, Ms. Tanaka provided students with the following prompt:

R Cinderella

A Yeh-Shen

F Letter

T Our sisters

RAFT WRITING PROMPTS

R – your Role as a writer

A – the Audience to whom you are writing

F – the Format of your writing

T – the Topic on which you are writing

Figure 4.2

Following the reading of *Rough-Face Girl* (Martin, 1992), Ms. Tanaka developed two different writing prompts, based on the last names of students:

	Letters A – M	Letters N – Z
Role	Cinderella	Yeh-Shen
Audience	Rough-face girl	Rough-face girl
Format	Letter	Letter
Topic	Our sisters	Our sisters

In this case, Ms. Tanaka only changed the role, specifically to learn whether or not students identified different perspectives from two different versions of Cinderella. Over time, they also discussed the reasons why men came to the rescue in all of the books and students were invited to create alternative endings in which Cinderella rescues herself.

If you are interested in social sensitivity for yourself, it may be worthwhile to try out the "Reading the Mind in the Eyes" test which can be found at the following web address: socialintelligence.labinthewild.org/mite/. This is a well-used measure of our ability to understand and work with others. It aims to measure your ability to accurately interpret the emotional states of others by viewing pictures of just their eyes (Baron-Cohen et al., 2001). It is a high predictor of both the individual success of working in groups, and the collective ability to understand and work with others as a predictor of the groups' success, particularly on challenging tasks. See how you do. It may just help convince you that teaching social sensitivity to your students is worth the time.

Unlike many birds, bees, and fish, we humans have not evolved the natural ability to form real-time closed-loop cues to swarm. John and Shirley wanted a swarm of starlings (called a murmuration) on the front cover of their feedback book, with the implicit message that feedback needs to be reciprocal between the giver and receiver, and both need to sometimes work together to understand and advance the subtle variations in the learning occurring around them. Flocking birds detect high-speed motions through the murmuration, and swarming bees generate complex body vibrations called a "waggle dance" that encodes information. We need to help students swarm, and buzz, to be vigilant to learning when with others, and to see the group as "multiple eyes" to help move the group forward. Young and colleagues (2013) investigated the starling's "remarkable ability to maintain cohesion as a group in highly uncertain environments and with limited, noisy information." They found that the birds use information from the six to seven birds nearest them and this led to optimizing a trade-off between group cohesion and individual effort (a hint to Chapter 7 on group size). More than this number requires additional sensory and cognitive effort and starts to be unreliable and break the murmuration.

Learning From a Distance

Group size is equally important in distance learning. For younger students, partners are often used to ensure that students have opportunities to take turns, speak and listen, and focus on their partner. As they get older, group size tends to increase. Importantly, students need to understand the task and their role in completing the task.

Potency

When we introduced social sensitivity, we noted that there were two dominant skills needed for collective student efficacy to flourish. We discussed the first, now to the second. As Lee et al. (2011) noted, group effectiveness is influenced by three factors: task interdependence (how closely *group* members work together), outcome interdependence (whether, and how, *group* performance is rewarded), and *potency* (members' belief that the *group* can be effective). We explore task interdependence in Chapter 5 of this book and we will focus on outcome interdependence via rewards and assessment of the group in Chapter 8. Now it's time to turn our attention to potency.

The concept of group potency was proposed by Shea and Guzzo (1987) as a key determinant of team effectiveness. They define potency as "the collective belief of *group* members that the *group* can be effective" (p. 26). Although there are many parallels between potency and team-efficacy, a critical point of departure is that potency refers to generalized beliefs about the capabilities of the team across tasks and contexts (i.e., our team will be successful no matter what the task). In contrast, team efficacy is more of a positive evaluation of the capacity of the team to accomplish the goal. "We will succeed" compared with "we can succeed." For example, members of a team might believe that they can design a specific new product (high team-efficacy) but might not believe that they can effectively produce, market, and sell the product (low potency). The higher the potency, the more positive were the collective outcomes.

Guzzo, Yost, Campbell, and Shea (1993) suggest that there are external and internal factors that influence potency (see Figure 4.3). As they note, these factors are always at play when groups come together to complete a task. As educators, we can consider both the external and internal factors as we form groups and construct tasks. We have already discussed many of these already in this section. We have focused on vicarious learning experiences and persuasion as well as the role that goals can play in group learning.

When Michael Woo learned about the contributors to potency, he decided that he needed to develop student leadership with the groups. Mr. Woo teaches mathematics to high school students and notes that many times students come to algebra and geometry with the belief that they are not good at mathematics and that they can't learn mathematics. As he says, "This anti-math mindset has to be confronted and I think one of the best ways to do that is to have students work together to see that they can be successful. When the collective is effective, individuals will start to recognize their role in the groups' success."

Mr. Woo identified ten students in his first period class to test his idea that leadership was a missing piece for developing potency and subsequently collective student efficacy. These were not the top performing students in the class, but rather students who seemed to have followers in the class or school. He asked the students to meet him after school for a quick conversation. During their meeting, Mr. Woo asked the students to define what it meant to be a leader. Most of them agreed that it was to get others to follow. Mr. Woo said to this group of students, "If that is your definition, then you're all already leaders. Others already follow you. But I'm thinking

A MODEL OF POTENCY

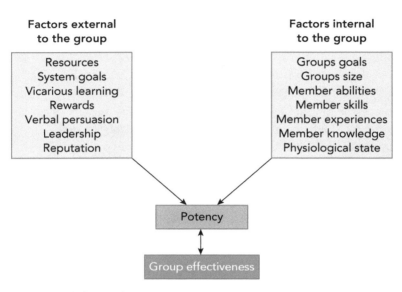

Factors external to the group

Resources
System goals
Vicarious learning
Rewards
Verbal persuasion
Leadership
Reputation

Factors internal to the group

Groups goals
Groups size
Member abilities
Member skills
Member experiences
Member knowledge
Physiological state

Potency

Group effectiveness

Source: Guzzo, R., Yost, P., Campbell, R., & Shea, G. (1993). Potency in groups—articulating a construct. *British Journal of Social Psychology, 32,* 87–106.

Figure 4.3

that leadership is even more than that. I think it's about motivating people to achieve something, like a common goal. I think you have to be able to both inspire and support. Would any of you be willing to serve as group leaders in our class for the next month?"

Kiara was the first to respond, "I mean, well yes, but I'm terrible at math. I can't really support people if I don't know what I am doing. So, I think you picked the wrong person."

Mr. Woo responded, "You'll need to learn the math, along with all of the other students. But think about this. Does a leader always have to know everything before the people being led? Or can the leader learn along the way, while making sure everyone else is doing their part?"

Kiara nodded and said, "Yeah, I can see that. I'm willing to try." At that moment, all of the others agreed as well. Kiara clearly was an influential student. Over the next week, Mr. Woo provided this group of students with leadership tasks and short lessons. He met with them as a group while the other students completed independent tasks. These ten-minute sessions provided students with ideas for redirecting conversations, many of which came from a colleague who worked in the technology department (for further ideas see www.iltsa.org/National_TSA_Leadership_Lessons.pdf).

The following week, Mr. Woo reorganized the groups and had one of the ten new leaders placed in each group. He informed the class that they would be tackling a very difficult problem together. He noted that he had assigned temporary leaders for each group but that everyone had to engage in learning and everyone had to be able to explain the thinking of the group. Here was their task:

> The drama club is holding a fundraiser BBQ in order to purchase new costumes. They put together a plate lunch featuring BBQ chicken, baked beans, potato salad, and a roll. Based on data from past fundraisers, they learned that when they charged $4.00 for the plate, they sold 120 plates. When they charged $4.50, they sold 110 plates. Assuming this trend continues, how much should they charge per plate to maximize their total earnings?

The leaders in each group got started. They knew that their role was to invite each person in their group to share initial thoughts. They then moved to problem solving and invited members of the group to share their thinking, modeling, and demonstrating as they did. Over the next twenty-five minutes, groups solved the problem and retaught parts of their thinking to their peers. They worked to ensure that each member of each group could explain the thinking behind their answers.

With ten minutes remaining in the class period, Mr. Woo told the class that they would now complete an individual task that would require them to apply what they had learned. The problem was similar but with different variables and figures. To a student, they could explain the thinking that led to their recommendations. On the way out of the door, Kiara said, "Yeah, that was pretty cool. I think our group can solve anything that you throw at us."

Mr. Woo knew that he needed to develop more leaders with the class and that over the year the role needed to be assigned to everyone in the class. But simply focusing on leadership skills allowed him to develop the potency of the group and change their belief systems about the roles they could play in learning.

Of course, students may need to develop skills or receive support in any of the external or internal factor areas. Having said that, without the factors that contribute to potency, we're not sure that collective student efficacy can really develop. And if it does not, students may be working with peers and either not learning or not seeing the benefit from this arrangement. The old adage, you have to go slow to go fast, seems to apply here. There are a lot of "I" and "We" skills that students need to develop if they are going to benefit from the power of the collective. And when those skills are developed, they learn more and develop ways of being that will serve them well throughout their lives.

Learning From a Distance

As some students work independently or on asynchronous tasks, you can meet with students in smaller groups to develop their leadership skills. For example, in their fourth-grade class, Brianna Kerr-White had her students work on a writing task in the waiting room. Students were still logged into the video conference, but they were working independently. She invited six students from the waiting room into the main room as they would be tasked with leading the discussion in breakout rooms. Ms. Kerr-White provided the student leaders with sentence frames to encourage peers to talk, ideas for refocusing the group, and a rubric for peer review of writing. Each student was asked to explain one line of the rubric to the others in the leadership group to ensure that they all understood what they would be doing. Ms. Kerr-White rotates student leaders and makes sure that they are prepared for their role before sending them into breakout rooms.

The "I" and the "We" Skills

Bringing some skills to a group and then leaving the group experience having learned and been successful is reinforcing for all of the students involved. It reinforces the value of the individual skills as well as the belief that learning is enhanced when interaction opportunities are utilized. Interacting with others in the group also builds and reinforces skills, specifically the "we" skills, that students can take with them to the next group. In essence, the "I" and "We" skills continue to develop as students learn how to learn as well as how to engage with others.

Sometimes, students' collaborative learning is compared with a sports team. Although it is true that sports teams rely on "I" and "We" skills, many do not: The analogy only goes so far. In basketball or cricket, if the team wins, everyone wins. Each player uses their individual skills to the best of their ability, but when the team wins, every player is credited with a win, irrespective of the number of errors made or the fact that some players contributed very little. Of course, there are individual statistics for each player, based on their position, that can be compared with other individuals' scores. In school, it is rare to have a "group win" academically. Unlike many sports, most academic tasks are not "won" as a group. Everyone is expected to understand the text that Ms. Lowe used, and everyone is expected to master the division of fractions. The sports analogy only goes so far in helping us think about building collective student efficacy.

Unlike in many sports, in school groups the goal is that everyone attains a specific level of understanding of the content. Some students know more at the outset of the lesson and some students have stronger literacy and numeracy skills. Thus, in school, the goal of the collaborative phase of learning is to develop and reinforce the "I" skills while also preparing students for future roles in society in which the "we" skills will be critical. The core business of collective student efficacy is working with students to build their personal identity inside a team, to have confidence they can contribute, and to build the belief that the group can be more successful than any one individual. Our students, more and more, will be asked to work in groups as contributors, translators, communicators, and critics, and thus need awareness and clarity on how to work in groups as strategic and capable team members.

CHAPTER 5

THE LEARNING DESIGN OF THE LESSON

What types of learning happen better and more quickly in groups? When can we harness the power of the collective to accelerate student learning? This chapter focuses in on what conditions need to exist within tasks to have the best outcomes when students work together. We first outline four definitions of task that can be considered, differentiated by their goals, assessment, and responsibilities. We then use these definitions to describe the various examples of tasks and lessons throughout this book.

The Four Key Task Designs for Collective Student Efficacy

If we look at task design, motivation can be varied, according to *the goal, the assessment*, and the *type of task*. Table 5.1 describes the different types of collective tasks (Steiner, 1972). The second column contains our own version of these labels. Note that many of the examples from physical school can be adapted for distance learning. The examples in the distance learning column have been used effectively while students learn remotely.

In such classifications, it is common to include "disjunctive" tasks as well, but we exclude them as they describe tasks where only one member of the group needs to perform effectively for the team to succeed.

COLLECTIVE TASKS

Nature of Tasks	Our Version	Description	Examples From Physical School	Examples From Distance Learning
Additive	Many hands make light work	Requires member resources to be summed for productivity and the performance exceeds that of the best member	Brainstorming research topics; Jigsaw reading	Student-generated sample test questions; WebQuest (students research and share with each other to produce their product)
Compensatory	Merging all skills	Where contributions are pooled by agreement, any errors can be corrected by others, and the performance should be better than most individual members' performance	Numbered heads together; think-pair-share; reciprocal teaching	Five-word summaries (partners agree on five words and then join another partnership to agree on five words from the original ten); Internet Reciprocal Teaching
Conjunctive	All must be perfect, or we lose	Requires all members to perform effectively and where performance can be affected by the worst member	Group exams; competitive debate; table points	Group projects without individual accountability; speed, timed, or competitive learning tasks
Discretionary	Combining any way we want	Where resources can be combined in any way and performance decided by majority	Creating a group PowerPoint presentation; group summaries	Problem-based learning tasks

Table 5.1

If collective student efficacy is our goal, a critical decision is to ensure that the tasks assigned to students

a) have an appropriate challenge and motivation factor so that more than one thinker is required and there is enthusiasm to work together to solve a particular problem;

b) are more open than closed to allow for multiple interpretations;

c) allow for enough apparent knowledge for the task to be achievable by all;

d) have appropriate clarity about skills and knowledge (or knowing that and knowing how) within the tasks;

e) are built so that errors and mistakes are seen as opportunities for all to learn and able to be attended to without shame, leading to interdependence and connection between the students so that individuals and the group experience success and attain mastery.

Assessment is dealt with in Chapter 9, but clearly the form the teacher's judgment takes will impact students' motivation to work together—and such constructive alignment between the goals of the task, the task design, the criteria of success, and the assessments is critical to success in classes but particularly to develop collective student efficacy.

The Challenge and Motivation Factor

Teams are valuable when they are used to a) ensure students are progressing toward meeting transfer level content and skill demands by addressing a challenging task and b) developing collaborative knowledge and skills to engage in team environments that address challenging tasks (McDowell, 2019). If the task set is too easy, requires no discussion or pooling of ideas or strategies, or is too boring, students are unlikely to collaborate or engage with energy and enthusiasm. If tasks are too hard, some students might lack the confidence to learn and be less likely to contribute. Tasks should be not too easy, not too hard, and not too boring.

In *Developing Expert Learners*, McDowell (2019) also emphasizes the importance of students having their ideas challenged during discussions

Tasks should be not too easy, not too hard, and not too boring.

to deepen their understanding. Teachers should take care to not interrupt the flow but to create pause moments for the whole class in which ideas so far are summarized and then challenged, not only by the teacher but maybe from other groups:

> The key strategy to focus on to ensure functional teams and effective group decisions is to allow for dissent and to encourage well thought-out arguments and sustained debate. Teachers may have a tendency to keep their opinions to themselves [. . .] but [. . .] offering up a conflicting idea or argument is often the most important step to reaching an efficacious decision. Challenging prior misconceptions or biases is often a necessary strategy in developing better collective solutions that incorporate multiple perspectives, experiences, and shared learning. (p. 60)

Repeated success (mastery) is the most significant source of collective efficacy because it draws on firsthand experiences rather than the opinion of others (Bandura, 1977). Pink (2011) defined mastery as "the desire to get better and better at something that matters." Rather than motivation coming first, followed by success, it is in fact more likely to be the other way around: **Experience success and your self-efficacy starts to build, encouraging you to think that you could probably achieve success again.** Success leads to increased motivation, leading to further success. Donohoo and Katz (2019) describe key features of teacher environments which lend themselves more readily to pupil mastery experiences and those that lend themselves to pupil performance, so the culture of teaching and teachers in a school directly impacts whether students are more likely to be mastery or performance driven.

Success leads to increased motivation, leading to further success.

Open Tasks Lead to Collective Engagement

To make tasks challenging, motivating, yet achievable, they need to have an end goal, but one in which the means to get there is not obvious or has many possible routes to success (e.g., How many different shapes can you draw with an area of 24 sq. cm.?). Some goals might even have no right or wrong answers but require ideas to be pooled and debated (e.g., decide the qualities of a true friend or decide how best to spend $1,000 to improve your school with justifications). These are considered more "open" than "closed" tasks. It is the taught interdependence skills which come into play during these tasks, to ensure that everyone is involved productively, respected for their views, and on task.

MASTERY VS. PERFORMANCE ENVIRONMENTS

Mastery environments	Performance environments
There is an open-to-learning stance	There is a knowing stance
There is an orientation toward mastery goals	There is an orientation toward performance goals
Teams engage in joint work characterized by positive interdependence	Teachers work in isolation
Progress is monitored based on success criteria	Performance is monitored in relation to how well others are doing

Source: Donohoo & Katz, 2019.

Table 5.2

Learning From a Distance

These types of questions are especially useful in distance learning. Inviting groups to discuss these types of questions builds their communication and interaction skills, while allowing them to share their thinking. For example, you might ask "Would you rather leave your hometown never to return or never leave your hometown?" Or perhaps, "Would you rather have breakfast for dinner or dinner for breakfast?" As students develop norms for their interactions online, the questions can become more focused on the content of the class.

Challenging tasks have an end goal in which the means to achieve it is not obvious and/or has many possible routes to success.

Closed tasks, on the other hand, have one right answer and usually one route to success (e.g., find the area of this circle), and are unsuitable for group discussion. With closed tasks, the problem could be solved by either all students individually or, as part of a group, the student with the quickest right answer will necessarily be the only one to do the thinking.

The following description is an open task, which was given to eleven-year-olds, with a correct answer but no specific method to find it. Many students can race through multiplication "sums" easily but without knowing why they are following the rules of the procedure. When they come to solve a real-life problem with multiplication, they can end up not knowing which calculation to use. Mathematics needs practice in applying the rules as well as mastering them, which led to this teacher presenting her class with a problem which needed a multiplication solution.

Notice the importance of the paired ownership and the teacher's intervention.

MATH PROBLEM SOLVING (NINE-TO-ELEVEN-YEAR-OLDS) WORKING IN PAIRS

The teacher's aim for this lesson was "To understand that multiplication is repeated addition." Because the task was presented as a problem to solve—to see whether the students could come up with a solution which demonstrated their understanding of repeated addition—this was not the learning intention given at first to the class. Students were told their learning intention was: "To solve a mathematical problem."

By the end of the lesson, when repeated addition had been discovered and discussed, the specific learning intention of knowing that multiplication is repeated addition was made explicit and made more meaningful because it had been used in a practical problem rather than given as a mathematical fact without context.

Type of Task: COMPENSATORY (merging all skills)

Task: Imagine you have a large bag of pennies. How many will fit edge to edge, covering as much space as possible, over your entire desk? You can have two pennies to help you . . .

As this could be solved in different ways, the success criteria focus on transferable problem-solving strategies rather than telling the students exactly how to solve it. These "problem solving" success criteria can be displayed as a poster for every time problem solving comes up in math lessons:

Problem solving success criteria:	Talk partner success criteria:
Remember to:	
• Make an estimate/prediction of the answer	• Hold eye contact
• Underline the important words in the problem	• Look interested
• Decide which resources might help you	• Don't get distracted

• Decide what to do first and see what happens	• Think about what your partner is saying
• Change strategies if you need to	• Be prepared to change your mind
• Check answers in a different way (e.g. calculator)	• Don't interrupt or talk over each other
• Compare your answer with your prediction	• Be helpful and polite
	• Use sentence stems (I agree / I disagree because . . .)

Notes

This is an open-ended problem, which reveals how far students know that multiplication is repeated addition (numbers of rows totaled). Often students know a routine algorithm without fully understanding the mathematical concept behind it.

The teacher, Angela Evans from a Wisconsin elementary school, observed two eleven-year-old students, Jake and Sandeep, tackling this task and noted every step in their problem solving but also in the interdependence and cooperation:

Jake & Sandeep's actions	Interdependence and cooperation
1. They first decided together to use the two coins, jumping one over the other to count how many fitted along the width and then the length of the table.	Both at once saw that with two coins they could count the length and width and agreed on this strategy.
2. Jake wrote down the answers (nineteen and forty) while Sandeep got a calculator. They multiplied the numbers and wrote down the answer. Then Jake said to Sandeep, "Try forty divided by nineteen." He did this. They then tried adding the two numbers.	They agreed they'd need a calculator so they divided the tasks. Neither was convinced that 760 was the right answer, so the second calculation was readily agreed on.
3. The teacher asked what they had done so far. They replied, "We know it's one of these, but we don't know which one." They had discussed this and come to a dead end. Although they were very good at long multiplication, I now knew they had no idea that multiplication is repeated addition.	Their mutuality was evident. They needed teacher intervention.

(Continued)

(Continued)

Jake & Sandeep's actions	Interdependence and cooperation
4. Ms. Evans asked them to try another way to find out. The students first tried the ever-decreasing perimeters. They started to see that the middle zone was not going to work, so agreed to get a meter ruler and try measuring the table.	Teacher intervention, not giving answers but suggesting they find another way. They were still resolved and confident that they would find a solution! They worked well together trying to draw round the coins to ensure maximum coverage of the table, taking one coin each.
5. They came to a dead end again and I suggested they imagine that they now had a whole bag of coins and I asked, "What would be the best way of arranging those coins on the table?"	Teacher intervention—suggesting they think about the original problem, not giving answers.
6. The light came on for both students at once as they said "Rows!"	Eureka!
7. They continued the task together, one recording, one counting, and eventually got to the right answer, without doing a long multiplication sum. They realized that they had to count rows but failed to create a standard multiplication sum. Instead they wrote forty, nineteen times in a column, then proceeded to count up the 40s until they had 760.	They shared the task: Jake excitedly wrote the list of 40s, while Sandeep mentally calculated by adding pairs of 40s. Their excitement was tangible as they realized they were close to the answer.
8. I asked them to look back at their calculator findings from the beginning of the problem and they realized it was the same answer. They had together, by trying different strategies and ideas, discovered what long multiplication actually is!	There was joint reflection on the fact that repeated rows were in fact long multiplication. They were aware of what had been learned and had worked together with enthusiasm and motivation. The key learning was to realize that they could have used their quick column method of calculation rather than a long list of numbers.

Ensuring That Students Have Sufficient Knowledge, Confidence, and Motivation to Tackle the Task

There is always the dilemma about when to focus on the content, the subject-matter vocabulary, and the major ideas and when to focus on relating these ideas, problem solving, and allowing students to take some direction in the learning to the goals. Of course, this choice does not have to be a binary, but it is too often the case that some students are left behind because they do not have sufficient knowledge to bring to, to contribute to, to critique when in, and to address the goals of the group.

Many have heard of the fourth grade "reading slump" when the early gains of learning to read stop—as students are asked to be more involved in comprehending, understanding, and inferring from reading. But as we and others have shown (Pfost et al., 2014) this is less a "slump" than it is teachers presuming students already have the subject matter vocabulary and necessary knowledge prior to the deeper tasks. This assumption leads to leaving behind those students who lack this necessary surface level knowledge to understand, use to make connections, and apply in problem situations. This prior knowing is even more critical when students are asked to work in groups—it is safe to assume that not every child will bring equal knowledge and understanding to the group, and if this prior knowledge is not dealt with, we can safely guarantee that not every child will gain from being in the group.

We have developed a model that may help in the understanding of this learning cycle, in the planning needed for each part of the cycle, and in the evaluation of where to best move next to achieve success. Hattie and Donoghue (2016) identified four hundred plus learning strategies, and then completed a meta-synthesis (228 meta-analyses from 18,956 studies and between thirteen and twenty million students) to identify which and when these strategies were more effective to advance learning. It turned out that one learning strategy can be effective at one point in the learning cycle, but this same strategy might not be so effective at other points. Hence the development of the model to help explain this variance.

Hattie and Donoghue's work acknowledges that students bring three major sets of learning attributes to the class (they also bring factors prior to these three such as poverty, cultural values, health, and parental expectations, to name a few). They call these three attributes the "skill," "will," and "thrill":

1. The skill—prior achievement, working memory, culture, and home,

2. The will—dispositions such as resilience or emotional strength, resourcefulness, or cognitive capabilities, reflection or strategic awareness, relating, or social sophistication, and

3. The thrill—motivations such as to master, to pass the test, compliance, look good in front of friends

These inputs are also among the three most critical learning *outcomes* as well.

To help explain the variability in the findings of their meta-synthesis, the Visible Learning Strategies model included two major moderators in their model—the first was whether the focus of the instruction was surface ("knowing *that*" knowledge; e.g., facts, ideas), deep ("knowing *how*" understanding; e.g., relations between ideas), and transfer (both near and far, to new problems and situations). The second was whether students are being first exposed to the learning and in the phase of acquiring surface or deep knowing, and consolidating these ideas or relations (see Figure 5.1). Some strategies were differently effective depending on when they were used in this instructional cycle. For example, memorization had an effect-size of .03 when used in the surface acquiring phase, but .73 in surface consolidating; problem-based learning had an effect of .14 for surface and .50 for deep learning.

They identified some powerful strategies worth teaching students, but the skill of knowing when to apply them (part of self-regulation) can be difficult, which is why the cognitive attributes of the task need to be carefully considered by teachers to help students. Besides the learning intentions and success criteria, teachers need to consider the knowledge, skills, and optimal learning strategies needed to attain these goals. We can determine these strategies by watching, interviewing, and listening (e.g., getting students to think aloud) into how students think while doing tasks. This feedback to the teacher is not easy to acquire, as we need to be able to hear both successful and not successful thinking, but it is powerful to improve the lesson and know what to re-teach.

HATTIE AND DONOGHUE (2016) MODEL OF LEARNING PHASES

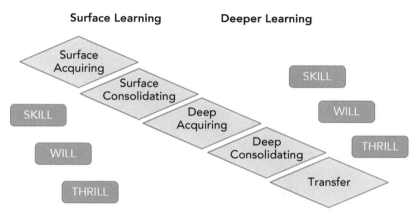

Source: Hattie and Donoghue, 2016.

Figure 5.1

The most effective strategies include: outlining and summarizing when first acquiring surface knowledge; deliberate practice, practice testing, rehearsal and memorization, seeking and receiving feedback, and distributed practice when consolidating surface knowledge; relating and meta-cognition, and seeking clarity when deep acquiring; self-verbalizing with peers and teachers when consolidating deep learning; and detecting similarities and differences when in transfer learning (see Table 5.3).

Let's consider an example. The students in Sonia Ruiz's sixth grade class were assigned research papers. They could select a topic, based on their investigation of the human body. Ms. Ruiz provided students with many books, websites, videos, articles, and artifacts about the various human systems. Their first task was to read to develop their background knowledge on a system within the human body. They were to take notes and organize their understanding. Ms. Ruiz then grouped students based on the body systems that they had selected (e.g., respiratory, circulatory, nervous). The students then shared their notes and ideas with one another. They asked each other for help as they added

EFFECTIVE STRATEGIES AT EACH PHASE OF LEARNING

Phase of Learning	Effective Strategies for Individual Learning	Effective Strategies for Group Learning
Surface acquiring	Integrating with prior knowledge (d = .93) Outlining (d = .85) Mnemonic (d = .76) Working memory training (d = .72) Summarizing (d = .74) Organizing (d = .60) Underlining and highlighting (d = .44)	
Surface consolidating	Deliberate practice (d = .77) Rehearsal and memorization (d = .77) Seeking and receiving feedback (d = .71) Help seeking (d = .60) Spaced vs. massed practice (d = .60) Repeated reading (d = .75)	Jigsaw* (d = 1.20)
Deep acquiring	Elaboration and organization (d = .75) Strategy monitoring (d = .71) Metacognition strategies (d = .61) Study skills (d = .45) Concentration/persistence/engagement* (d = .54) Self-efficacy* (d = .71)	Perceived task value* (d = .46) Collaborative learning* (d = .34) Reciprocal teaching (d = .74)
Deep consolidating	Evaluation and reflection (d = .70) Discussing self-consequences (d = .70) Self-verbalizing & self-questioning (d = .64)	Seeking help from peers* (d = .83) Classroom discussion* (d = .82) Problem solving teaching* (d = .68)
Transfer	Detecting similarities and differences (d = 1.32) Seeing patterns to new situations (d = 1.14)	Peer tutoring (d = .51)

*Stage of initiation but continues into later stages

Table 5.3

to their own notes and worked to identify a topic and question. For example, in the nervous system group, Annaleah asked her peers if any one of them found information about pain. She said, "My grandma has a lot of pains, so I am thinking about learning about how the brain knows about pain." Several of her classmates offered her information from their notes, and Annaleah updated her own. Horacio asked if anyone learned about memory problems because his parents told him that his grandma had memory problems. As he said, "I didn't think about that for a topic until Annaleah talked about her grandma, but I wanna know about that." Albert said that he remembered seeing a book in the pile about memory and left the group to go get it. When he returned, he said, "See, here it is. Maybe this could help you. I want to know more about balance because I read about it on a website. Some people are really, really good at balance but not me. Did you find anything about that?" The group continues to share resources with each other, having created a list of topics. They commit to be on the lookout for information that others in their group can use.

As part of the task, students are asked to create an outline for their paper and then share their thinking aloud with their teacher before writing. As Ms. Ruiz says, "I like to meet with them as they start to finalize their research topics and hear their thinking. I also want them to understand that they are part of a group and need to teach each other what they learn about the specific system they have chosen. In fact, we have regular share sessions so that they can talk through their thinking with members of their group and ask each other questions. It helps them be more aware of their own thinking so that it's not just about the topic they are writing about but it becomes about the way that they think and solve problems."

As they complete their tasks, the students in Ms. Ruiz's class ask themselves and their peers a number of questions, ranging from content to strategies. They engage in many discussions as they share information and findings with each other. As part of their research project, the students note similarities and differences in how their peers share what they have been learning in writing. For example, Horacio said, "You two started with a question in your paper. But you (Annaleah) started with a personal story and you (Tony) started with a strong fact. I am still thinking about how to start. But they are all interesting to make your reader want to know more."

Over time, the students share their understanding about the particular system they have investigated with larger groups of students. Although most of the work was done outside of her class, she provided them time to interact with the peers during class. Ms. Ruiz uses a Jigsaw process at the end of each research paper so that students learn from each other and have an opportunity to learn content as well as tools for writing. As she says, "It's more than the content. I'm working to get them to develop some strong research skills that will apply to anything that they need to do. It's a way of thinking that I'm working on."

A major implication of this model is that there are some key phases we need to get right in our planning or learning design. We should not assume all students can apply the best strategies or even be aware that different strategies are best at different phases. Another implication is that there are optimal times for students to work collectively. In most cases, the optimal time for collective work is after they have acquired and consolidated surface-level content knowledge. Problem-based learning and many similar deeper teaching methods have much lower effects if the focus is content (.15) but much higher after it can be assured the students have sufficient content to start the problem phase (.50). Yes, problem-based learning can also attend to the content, but there are many other more effective methods such as deliberate teaching related methods. Methods such as class discussion, students thinking aloud, and Socratic questioning among students are best introduced in group and class after there is some assurance that the students have the knowledge to so engage in these deeper tasks.

Clarity About Knowledge and Skills: Knowing *That* and Knowing *How*

Learning intentions need to be clear, from overarching long term intentions to specific lesson learning intentions. Students might have a lesson in which they are learning to write a newspaper article (*skill or knowing how*) about the events of July 4, 1776 (*knowledge or knowing that*). These would be given as two separate learning intentions:

> ***We are learning to write a newspaper article***; and
> ***We are learning about the events of Independence Day***

Success criteria are most helpful for the students if they also focus on reminders of what they need to **include** to achieve success (i.e., a headline, a subheading, summary in the first paragraph, etc.) or **focus on** for the knowledge (e.g., remember to consider the following elements of Independence Day . . .). If the learning intention calls for students to demonstrate their knowledge in a well-practiced form (e.g., explaining), especially for secondary students, then the learning intention would simply state the knowledge content and the skill (of explaining for instance) would be assumed. An example of a knowledge-only learning intention might be the following:

> **We are learning to explain the impact of plastic on the environment.**

Learning From a Distance

Clarity about learning is critical in distance learning. In both synchronous and asynchronous lessons, students need to know both the knowledge of how and the knowledge of what. Without that, school becomes a series of tasks to check off. With this type of compliance, learning can be hindered.

The Connection Factor

Appropriate tasks for collective student efficacy rely on a safe culture of normalized error and respect for each other's views and opinions. If there is a culture of humiliation and shame, students are unlikely to take risks and expose errors in their thinking. It is the teacher's role to emphasize that we all learn from each other, having different strengths, characters, and skills which should be nurtured and sought after in order to pool our best ideas and strengthen each other's confidence in being able to contribute and add value. Interdependence starts with trust, of the teacher and also each other.

Interdependence starts with trust, of the teacher and also each other.

Collective efficacy is dependent upon *perceptions* regarding task interdependence, or how connected students are based on the tasks they are assigned. **The greater the task interdependency, the greater the collective efficacy**, so performance relationship is maximized. Some student tasks require very little interdependence while others require a high degree (see Table 5.4). The relationship between collective efficacy and team performance is maximized when there is greater positive interdependence amongst the members of the team. Gully et al. (2002, p. 827) noted that *"when the task and context encourage coordination, communication, and cooperation among members, team-efficacy is related more strongly to performance than when interdependence is low."*

EXAMPLE TASKS: LOW VS. HIGH INTERDEPENDENCE

Low Interdependence	High Interdependence
Create a group poster in which each person draws one example of how plants reproduce, and they are then stuck on to one large sheet of cardstock. *The poster might look good in the end, but there is very little interdependence required. This is instead a faux "group" task as the students work separately. The task might be a good idea, but not if you want interdependency!*	Discuss together whether it is right for animals to be kept in zoos and present your arguments for and against. Your roles will be recorder (to keep a record of the ideas and summarize), questioner (to ask questions which provoke or come from a different point of view), reporter (to report back, from the recorded summary, the ideas and conclusions of the group), and manager (to make sure everyone speaks and gives their opinions (e.g., "Mia—what do you think about that?"). *Each student has a role, but their success depends on the interdependence among the group members.*

Table 5.4

Katz-Navon and Erez (2005) showed that collective efficacy predicted group performance only when a highly interdependent task required group members to interact and coordinate their efforts. Where there were low levels of task interdependence, collective efficacy had no significant impact on group performance. In contrast, how students felt about their own individual capacity to achieve, or their self-efficacy, emerged as a meaningful construct that explained any successful performance when the task required only low interdependence. We will discuss success criteria for interdependence in Chapter 6.

The point of any paired or group work is to get students talking and explaining ideas to each other so that they are actively thinking and working toward group success. As interdependence is critical for collective efficacy to take place, the task needs to enable interdependence and not lend itself to students finding it easier and more efficient to work on their own or leaving all the work to be done by others.

A task which cannot function without interdependency is the Jigsaw Strategy (type of task: ADDITIVE and COMPENSATORY). The Jigsaw method (d = 1.20) is among the most powerful teaching strategies to promote collective student efficacy for groups, as it reinforces the importance of task interdependence (Darnon et al., 2012). In Jigsaw, working with others on complimentary material removes the basis for social comparison, which increases the focus on knowledge sharing and therefore increases learning (Butera et al., 2011). Just as in a jigsaw puzzle, each piece—each student's part—is essential for the completion and full understanding of the final product. If each student's part is essential, then each student is essential, and that is precisely what makes the strategy so effective (see Fisher et al., 2000). Jigsaw lends itself particularly to a piece of knowledge which needs to be learned by all, as all class members at some time have to share with other groups the knowledge or findings of their previous group. This leads to ensuring that the students have the knowledge, the subject matter vocabulary, and the main ideas, before venturing to link their ideas more deeply in their understanding, and be able to then transfer knowledge to new problems or issues—a rarity among most teaching methods.

"To ensure that students experience positive interdependence, teachers need to structure cooperative learning situations in which children learn the content and are responsible for ensuring that all group members succeed in the assigned task." (Costa & Kallick, 2009, p. 63)

Learning From a Distance

Jigsaw is also effective in distance learning. Most platforms allow teachers to group and regroup students in breakout rooms. For ease of movement, teachers typically use the rename function to add a letter and number to each student (e.g., A1, A2, A3, A4, B1-B4, C1-C4, D1-D4). If there are four parts to the reading, there may be groups A through D and E through H with the numbers five, six, seven, eight (thus two groups are reading the first part of the text). Then, when they are in expert groups, all of the As are together and all of the Bs are together and so on. The groups would talk about their section of the text. Then they move to their numbered groups, so the ones would be together as would the twos, fives and so on. These new groups would each share what they learned from their section of the text and take notes while others share their parts of the text. They would then move back to their original groups (As, Bs, Ds, etc.) and discuss how their part of the text fit in with the whole text.

AN EXAMPLE OF THE JIGSAW STRATEGY

Imagine a task where we have five readings based on the achievements and beliefs of the Ancient Egyptians (buildings, pharaohs, burials, homes, gods).

Make sure students know the big picture of all the steps, so that they know the purpose of the strategy and are fully committed to each step, knowing what comes next.

1. Sit at tables of about three to five. Agree who is A, B, C, D, and E within each table.

2. Person A on each table reads and makes notes on one of the elements (e.g., buildings); Bs do the same for pharaohs; Cs on burials, Ds on homes, and Es on gods. All have about twelve minutes. They are asked to find out anything they don't understand, need to know more, and identify big ideas in the text.

3. All the As then meet together, similarly the Bs, Cs, Ds, and Es to talk about the main messages (about fifteen to twenty minutes). The value here is that all students, regardless of their perceived achievement level, can teach and learn from each other about the content and ideas for each influence. They talk about what makes sense and what did not (thus learning from each other) and come up with a summary of the main ideas. They need to know that they will each have to report this summary back to their home group.

4. The students then return to their original home groups and report back, in turn, the major findings and understandings to the others. So now there are five sets of ideas and understandings for each group. The major purpose of this step is to see connections between the major ideas across the five influences.

5. The students then are given a relational task, such as to discuss how their individual pieces fit in with the bigger picture of the significance of the Ancient Egyptians and their achievements and beliefs. A task is usually set to apply their knowledge into a report/poster or similar.

6. Each group shares their major ideas and a whole class discussion is held to ensure that all understand the main themes underlying these five practices.

Interdependence is woven into the structure of Jigsaw, so there is far less possibility of social loafing. Being accountable and important to one's peer group, with this strategy, is a powerful driver and motivator. At each step, the students know that the success of their home group depends on their individual effort, so knowing how the whole strategy works in advance is critical. When they go back to their group at Step three, instead of students perhaps allowing more knowledgeable members of the group to just give the answers, each individual will be actively hanging on the words of any students who can illuminate unclear information, because this will be to their advantage when they return to their home group—individual strengths are welcomed as they strengthen the group as a whole.

One good way to show students how the strategy works might be to do a trial lesson taking a topic the students already know a lot about or something it would be easy for them to assimilate. Jigsaw is powerful because it leads to group success, and group success, in which every individual feels they have made a valuable contribution and had some tangible learning, builds collective student efficacy.

Teachers' reflections on individual and group work, with and without interdependence success criteria: Bangkok Patana School, Bangkok

Over several months, teachers across the primary grades experimented and observed their students in group tasks, given interdependence success criteria or not, working together or independently. Their reflections highlight the key issues of the need for interdependence, group size, and the power of the group.

Year one teachers (five- and six-year-olds)

On comparing individuals working alone to those in a group task:

"The children learning in collaborative groups mostly joined in with the learning to some level or at some point during the learning. Children learning individually who found it hard to lock on to learning did not know how to get started and didn't complete any learning. This suggests that learning collaboratively helps children to be involved in learning and to get unstuck.

"Both the groups of three seemed to have a strong, positive leader in each. This impacted positively on the efficacy and engagement of the whole group. Children who had been previously disengaged and struggled with collaborative learning were listening and engaging with their group. This raises the questions of group personalities and the importance of training in group skills.

"Compared to children in groups, independent learners, working alone, were either very successful or not at all. This supports our original theory that by collaborating, children can help each other stay focused and complete learning successfully."

Year two teachers (six- and seven-year-olds)

"The children working in groups managed to bring themselves back from distraction and re-engage in the task, whereas the children learning individually gave up and got stuck before the task was finished. Could this suggest that collaboration enabled the children to re-engage with the task and to keep each other accountable?"

In observing groups with or without interdependence success criteria:

"The majority of the children in the group without success criteria played some role in the activity and participated to some extent. In the beginning it was only half the group who were

(Continued)

(Continued)

actively engaging with the learning task, while the others were engaging only with the resources. But, as time went on, those students not participating could see others in the group learning together and experiencing success (vicarious experience) which drew them into engaging with the task.

"The children with interdependence success criteria showed signs of applying some of these (listening, trying to include others). This suggests that the success criteria helped them to think about effective collaboration skills.

"The groups with interdependence success criteria didn't always keep to them, but, when reminded, began to show seeds of collaborative behavior. This suggests that the success criteria helped them but they need further experiences and guidance to embed those learning habits.

"Many children reflected that they had been successful when they hadn't completed the learning or hadn't participated fully in their group. A next step could be to unpick what 'being successful' looks like."

At a later date, about five months later:

"Children's collaborative skills had significantly improved—this could have been partly because the children are more settled and know each other better but also because the group sizes were smaller (3-4 rather than 6) and therefore more manageable.

"A group of 3 seemed to be more effective than a group of 4."

Years three and four (seven-to-nine-year-olds) came to the same conclusions as teachers from Year one.

Year six (ten-to-eleven-year-olds)

"Overall the class displayed higher self-efficacy when working in a group.

"Some children struggled with the generation of ideas during the independent part of the task, so perhaps some children need to collaborate at the start of the activity to get ideas from other children.

"Smaller groups seemed to cooperate more than groups of 6, as there were fewer opinions to be negotiated."

From this one school study, it seems that the help students receive from others means they are more supported and likely to achieve than those left to work alone. They appeared to be more motivated to succeed when working together at a task and in small groups of three rather than the more unwieldy groups of six. It was also highlighted that students need to be explicitly taught interdependence skills.

CHAPTER 6

LEARNING INTENTIONS AND SUCCESS CRITERIA FOR COLLECTIVE STUDENT EFFICACY

The fundamentals underlying learning intentions have been around a long time in education. Indeed, the origin of the word "education" means to guide, and that begs the question: guide to where? And perhaps even more importantly, is this "where" somewhere worthwhile? For most of the 19th century, this destination was framed in terms of very general, high-level objectives, often interpreted in almost random fashion. More often than not, there were misalignments between the curriculum objectives, the teaching content, and the evaluation or assessment of these objectives.

Because of this misalignment, taxonomies were developed to focus on objectives, such as Bloom et al. (1956), Gagné (1968), Biggs and Collis (1982), Webb (2002), among many others. We are sure all readers will be familiar with Bloom (1956), although many will be less familiar with the important changes the Bloom team made to their taxonomy in 2001 (Anderson & Bloom, 2001), adding another dimension relating to the cognitive complexity. In our view, this was a critical addition and, indeed, we believe that the cognitive complexity additions are far more important than the arbitrary six classifications that are more widely known (remember, understand, apply, analyze, evaluation, and create). The types of knowledge included in the cognitive dimension follow:

- Factual Knowledge
  - Knowledge of terminology
  - Knowledge of specific details and elements

- Conceptual Knowledge
  - Knowledge of classifications and categories
  - Knowledge of principles and generalizations
  - Knowledge of theories, models, and structures

- Procedural Knowledge
  - Knowledge of subject-specific skills and algorithms
  - Knowledge of subject-specific techniques and methods
  - Knowledge of criteria for determining when to use appropriate procedures

- Metacognitive Knowledge
  - Strategic knowledge
  - Knowledge about cognitive tasks, including appropriate contextual and conditional knowledge
  - Self-knowledge

Each of these levels of knowledge can be used to guide the development of learning intentions, success criteria, and assessments.

We avoid the term formative "assessment" as this encourages many educators to focus on tests and exams. We prefer the term *formative evaluation* as it privileges the many sources of evidence and the importance of "interpretation" of this evidence that can be used by teachers and students in the process of understanding where they are, where they need to be, and the success of the progression from there to here. Formative evaluation is "all those activities undertaken by teachers, and/or their students to modify teaching and learning activities in which they [the students] are engaged" (Black & Wiliam, 1998, p. 8). It means working with students so that learners know where they are in their learning, where they need to be, and how they are going to get there. It was this bringing of intention, the nature of success, and the how of learning, which led to the notions of learning intentions, success criteria, and responsive teaching to reduce the gap between where the students started to where they needed to be.

Learning Intentions

It is common practice today to share learning intentions with students where the expected learning behind the tasks and activities is revealed. It is essential that students understand the learning intentions and have clarity, so that they are able to hold a concept similar to that of the teacher (Sadler, 1989). Writing good learning intentions, though, is hard as we need to distinguish clearly in our planning not only what the students will be *doing*, but what they will be *learning* by doing it.

Sadler (1989) was emphatic about the importance of communicating standards (success criteria) to students up front. He argued students needed to know what constitutes quality and noted that this can be accomplished via worked examples of end points, descriptive statements, and scoring rubrics with teachers' qualitative comments.

Without this means-ends analysis, students can quickly believe learning in school is compliance. In far too many places, students define learning as doing tasks, handing them in on time, neat and preferably long, and their conceptions or misconceptions about learning and quality become irrelevant to the teacher. No wonder, close to 60 percent of students by the end of primary school do not find enjoyment in undertaking the tasks assigned by teachers. Engagement in learning should not be defined by what students do (whether they do it well or not) as in many cases there is not much learning in doing.

There are any number of resources about learning intentions and success criteria (e.g., Clarke, 2021; Fisher, Frey, Amador, & Assof, 2018). The claim here is that we need learning intentions and success criteria at both the individual and at the collective level. Successful collective learning entails a set of structures that help groups achieve a specific goal (Panitz, 1999). Collective efficacy is unlikely to materialize out of thin air. Rather, it needs structures to be put in place by the teacher. But collective student efficacy also develops from beginning steps, such as becoming familiar with success criteria and the rules for successfully working together, experiencing success, and enjoying the shared learning and social endeavor, so that confidence and expertise grows. The intentions and nature of success for students working in groups needs to be transparent and constructively aligned with the tasks, the teaching, and the assessments.

Clear academic and social goals with success criteria, along with appropriate tasks, help students not only achieve a specific goal, but also want

Writing good learning intentions, though, is hard as we need to distinguish clearly in our planning not only what the students will be doing, but what they will be learning by doing it.

We need learning intentions and success criteria at both the individual and at the collective level.

to work cooperatively again, as their collective efficacy strengthens. The success of the group empowers the individual to believe they can contribute effectively again. This is the mastery effect in which success leads to a greater belief in one's ability, both within a group but also to feel more empowered to tackle learning alone.

Learning From a Distance

We cannot emphasize enough the importance of clear learning intentions and success criteria in distance learning. We did not say that students need to know what they are learning at the outset of the lesson but rather that they should know at some point. This applies to both synchronous and asynchronous learning events. Interactive videos, live sessions, and even practice work should directly align with the expected learning intentions and help students understand what success looks like.

Robert Slavin (2010) argues that effective group work requires two criteria: a shared group goal and individual accountability. Without the former, with unclear goals, the group is like a ship without a rudder; without the latter, social loafing (Ringelmann, 1913) and dominant takeovers easily occur. Locke and Latham (2006) found that clear learning goals (such as, "to find out how to. . . .") are more motivating and lead to greater achievement than performance goals (such as "try to get an A grade"). They also found that goals are more motivating the more challenging they are, as long as they are still achievable. This is an important point. The learning intentions need to be challenging so that students choose to engage in the work required to achieve them. We mentioned this Goldilocks principle in Chapter 5 regarding tasks, and it applies to learning intentions, too: not too hard, not too easy, and not too boring.

It is clear that there needs to be both a) the academic learning intention and success criteria linked to an appropriate task as well as b) the success criteria for the social interaction required for collaboration and interdependence to be not only effective, but more effective than working on one's own and more likely to create individual skills needed for collective student efficacy to occur. The following example illustrates how the two can work together:

Design technology (ten-to-eleven-year-olds) working in groups of three or four	
Academic learning intentions and success criteria	**Social learning intentions and success criteria for interdependence**
Learning intention: I am learning to apply my knowledge of designing and building to new tasks **Learning intention**: I am learning about the different types of bridges, purposes, and construction techniques (knowledge) **Task:** Design and build a bridge using classroom material which will stand on its own. **Success criteria for applying taught design and technology knowledge** (transferable skill) Remember to: • Review your knowledge together • Design your product, using clear labels and measurements • Choose appropriate materials and tools • Test your design and decide together the successes and improvements needed • Redo or refine your collective design and test again **Knowledge about bridges** In your group consider: • The different types of bridges: beam, arch, truss, cantilever suspension and cable stay • The reasons for the different designs of the three Forth Bridges in Scotland • Shapes which provide strength in buildings and bridges • Stability and fixing solutions	**Learning intention**: We are learning how to collaboratively determine our successes and areas for improvement • Listen carefully without interrupting • Demonstrate that you value the ideas and opinions of others • Think about what is being said • Ask and answer questions. • Ensure that everyone has an opportunity to share • Work to reach consensus and identify places where we don't agree • Make decisions that are fair

Learning Intentions and Success Criteria

Clarity of purpose is essential, so clear learning intentions are a prerequisite of any learning, including collaborative activities. Learning intentions can be long term (the flow of electrons in circuits) or short term, lasting one or more lessons (Ohm's laws or closed loops). They can also describe knowledge (to know the causes of the Vietnam War) or a transferable skill (to attribute sources that support claims). Knowledge tends to start at the surface stage. Then, when that knowledge is compared to similar or contrasting knowledge, understanding deepens. When transferable skills are used to apply the knowledge in different contexts, learning is usually at the transfer and self-regulation stage. Skills and knowledge are often used together (write an argumentative essay with evidence in which you support a claim about the most significant cause of the Vietnam War) in which the generic skill of being able to write a newspaper report is used to apply that knowledge. Knowledge has often been marginalized in favor of skills. Both need equal status, as in the following example:

(Skill) Learning intention: We are learning to express our opinion in a formal letter

(Knowledge) Learning intention: We are learning about the effects of plastic on the environment

Context: The use of plastic packaging in the school cafeteria

Skill: We are learning to express our opinion in a formal letter (transferable skill)	Knowledge: We are learning about plastic use in food packaging (for this lesson only)
Remember to include: • The correct format for letters (addresses, salutations, closing, etc.) • Formal sentence starters (e.g., I am writing to inform you . . .) • A clearly stated opinion • Reasons for your opinion • If appropriate, acknowledgment of other opinions	Remember to include: 1. Evidence about the effects of plastic in the environment (e.g., recycling issues, use of fossil fuels, wildlife, pollution) 2. Examples of unnecessary packaging in school cafeteria 3. Biodegradable alternatives

The knowledge, in the second column, divided into the different elements, is simply a list of activity prompts, which most teachers automatically either tell students or provide them with a resource which contains the key facts for this topic or focus, such as a knowledge organizer (one sheet of key facts, key people, key events, etc.). The point is to make sure there is equal focus between the skill and the knowledge being applied in some way.

In addition to the learning intentions, students need to know what it means to have learned something. Success criteria (effect size .88) provide students with an idea of the destination for their learning and help students understand how to achieve the learning intention. Sometimes success criteria focus on process steps or ingredients needed. Other times, they focus on the performance outcome. Some skills, such as grammar (e.g., use of regular and irregular verbs) and punctuation (e.g., to let readers know when a character is talking), and many mathematical procedures have compulsory ingredients (rules), whereas others (e.g., to explain the development of a character) have a menu or toolkit of possible inclusions (tools), as in the following examples:

Rules skill (compulsory ingredients)	Toolkit skill (menu of possibilities)
L.I. To translate a ratio into a percentage	L.I. To write a story opening
Remember to:	Choose all or some:
• Identify the ratio, x:y (e.g., 8:25)	• Setting: dialogue, description, end at beginning
• Convert the ratio into a fraction, x/y (e.g., 8/25)	• Hook the reader: show, not tell; suggest what might happen or have happened
• Multiply the fraction by 100 (e.g., 8/25 x 100 = 32)	• Use senses
• Add the percentage sign (e.g., 32%)	• Create powerful images for the reader

Recall from earlier in this chapter that Sadler (1989) suggested that success criteria could include examples of end points, descriptive statements, and scoring rubrics with teachers' qualitative comments. There are many ways to communicate success criteria. Simply said, when students understand the criteria for success, they are more capable of achieving the learning intention. Let's explore a range of ways that this might look. For the learning intention, "We are learning how character development impacts plot," consider the ways to depict success criteria noted in Figure 6.1, depending on the type of task. These examples come from a class focused on *Pride and Prejudice* by Jane Austen.

EXAMPLES OF SUCCESS CRITERIA BY TASK TYPE

	"I Can" Statements	"Rules"	"Tools"
Task	Write a paragraph or record a video analyzing the impact of Mr. Darcy's letter on Elizabeth.	Show how Austen uses minor characters like Miss Bingley, Mr. Collins, and Lady Catherine De Bourgh to bring Elizabeth and Darcy together.	Write an alternate story ending for *Pride and Prejudice* in response to the question, "What if Mr. Darcy didn't write the letter to Elizabeth—or it didn't reach her?"
Success Criteria	• I can summarize my thinking in a thesis statement. • I can use evidence from the text to support my thesis. • I can construct a coherent paragraph that remains focused on my thesis.	Remember to include: • A strong introductory paragraph. • A thesis statement summarizing your position. • Several paragraphs that maintain a consistent voice, tone, and focus. • Examples from the text to support your claims. • A concluding paragraph that summarizes your thinking and connects back to your thesis.	Consider: • Darcy's personality. • The impact of Elizabeth's words on his behavior. • The impact of pride, honor, and prejudice in Darcy's life. • The influence of society at the time. • The impact of other people's influence on Darcy.
Purpose of Success Criteria	Summarize success in a positive statement so that students will think positively about their success.	Ensure that students have an exact checklist of all features/skills that need to be included to achieve success.	Provide possible options that students can choose from when success can take multiple forms.

Figure 6.1

Thus far, we have focused on the individual, academic learning intentions and success criteria students must master. But for collective student efficacy to flourish, the success criteria must be expanded. The collective success criteria help students focus on their work together and make meaning from those experiences. As we have noted, collective efficacy requires both "I" and "we" skills. Thus, teachers need to define success at both the individual and collective level.

Learning From a Distance

One of the virtual class jobs that teachers have created is the "success reminder." That student periodically adds the success criteria to the chat to remind peers what success looks like. In addition, the success reminder notes when the class has achieved success and leads the celebration of the success.

Success Criteria for Effective Interdependence: The Link to Collective Student Efficacy

Nuthall (2007) famously recorded and analyzed the conversations between children in classrooms over time. When children are tasked with working together, we see the impact of *not* having clear co-constructed success criteria for interdependence. Here is one extract example from his book *The Hidden Lives of Learners*—focus on Tui:

Group task: to divide a chart into four quarters labeled northeast, southeast, southwest and northwest winds, and to describe in each quadrant the kind of weather associated with that wind.

Tui:	I'm doing it Rasta colors, OK? See theirs (looking at next group's chart), theirs is neat. Theirs will be better than ours. I don't want that to happen.
Tony:	Don't worry about coloring it in.
Tui:	If we don't put in the information, we'll never get it finished.
Tony:	OK then, well let's do it.

Tui:	I'm not writing anything.
Tony:	I'll write it down.
Tui:	No you won't.
	Tui goes to find relevant book for his group.
Tui:	Here, have a look at this book.
Kathy:	You get one square each. I'll decorate my square.
Tui:	Wait. I'm decorating them.
Kathy:	Do them in black and go around in blue.
Tui:	When we're finished I'm going to decorate it.
Kathy:	I'm going to decorate my own square.
Tui:	No you don't. I'm going to decorate all of them, thank you . . .

"Tui maintained his dominance over the others in a group despite the fact that he knew less than they did about the purpose of the activities or their curriculum content."

Takeovers, illustrated by Tui, or social loafing (leaving it all to others) are less likely to occur if both academic goals and interdependence success criteria are a consistently key feature of students' learning environment. It is the marriage of these that give students the tools they need to be able to confidently work together, each with a part and a voice, at a given, appropriate task. Siciliano (1999) determined the criteria for an ideal team member as four deceptively simple elements:

Do your part	Complete the tasks assigned to you
	Be willing to put in time necessary to complete your team assignment
	Ask if there is anything you can do
	Pull your own weight and do your share of the assignment
Share your ideas	Express your opinions
	Respond to other group members' ideas
Work toward agreement	Be open to other ideas, opinions, and perspectives
	Be willing to work together
	Work as a team (not just on an individual basis)
Keep a positive attitude	Maintain a sense of humor
	Be courteous
	Give feedback in the form of constructive criticism

Learning From a Distance

You can use the four elements from Siciliano as a self-assessment that students take and reflect upon as part of their tasks in the learning management system. For example, English teacher Ashley Campbell created a "quiz" that she gives every Friday. There are no right answers to the quiz. Instead, students rate themselves on each of the elements and then provide a rationale for their selections. As Ms. Campbell notes, "I want to normalize this so we take this quiz each week and think about the ways in which we worked together. I am not looking for inflated perceptions but rather honest reflections about how students engaged with their peers. When I see a trend, I can schedule additional time to join a group or to work with an individual student. The goal is that they see that their success is enhanced when they engage in tasks with others."

These four criteria can be used to construct success criteria for working in groups. Often, these success criteria are evergreen, meaning that they are used across many lessons and units. For example, a group of middle school science teachers developed success criteria for students to use when they were engaged in discussions. These included the following:

- I listen carefully without interrupting.

- I demonstrate that I value the ideas and opinions of others.

- I think about what is being said.

- I ask and answer questions.

- We ensure that everyone has an opportunity to share.

- We work to reach consensus and identify places where we don't agree.

- We make decisions that are fair.

Notice that there are some "I" skills and some "we" skills that are the focus of these lessons. In these classes, students self-assess following group discussions to determine their successes and areas of need. As one of the middle school science teachers noted, "We all agreed to start with these success criteria and then add to them as students mastered the skills. For example, we are going to add one more next week that says, 'I can take the perspective of another person in the group.' We want students to develop more social sensitivity so we're going to try that. Over time, we plan to focus more on the 'we' skills and the beliefs that students have in the power of the group. We are thinking about adding a success criterion that says, 'We reflect on the processes we used to solve problems.' That might help take our students to the next level in their collective efficacy."

In addition to these evergreen group success criteria, teachers can focus on specific social skills that groups need to practice and develop on their way to collective efficacy. For example, the students in Andrea Stein's third grade class were learning about the geographical features in their local region. Ms. Stein used snowballing, which is the term often used to describe an activity where students first discuss in pairs, then join another pair and share their thoughts. This can then continue to groups of eight, all sharing their ideas. This strategy works well when ideas need to be pooled to get the best of all ideas. Consider the learning intentions and success criteria:

Learning Intentions:

- I am learning about the geography of our community.
- We are learning how to build on the ideas of others.

Success Criteria:

- I can use the terms deserts, mountains, valleys, hills, coastal areas, oceans, and lakes in my responses.
- I can match the terms to specific locations in our community.
- I can listen to others and paraphrase what others say.
- I can add to what my peers say while staying on the same topic.
- We can strive to reach agreements and help each other understand the content.

Notice that both knowledge and skills are valued and that the skills include both "I" and "we." Together, they contribute to learning and the development of collective efficacy. Thus far, we have focused on the tasks and skills necessary for students to benefit from the power of collective efficacy. We have argued that the construction of appropriate tasks for group learning and the intentional instruction in individual and collective skills are necessary components. In this chapter, we added the idea of individual and collective learning intentions and success criteria. Now we are ready to turn our attention to the structures within classrooms that allows collective efficacy to thrive: group configurations, instructional strategies, and assessments.

CHAPTER 7

LEARNING IN PAIRS AND GROUPS

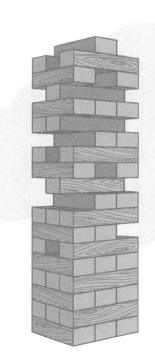

Thus far, we have focused on the skills students need to develop collective efficacy as well as the types of tasks that foster this kind of learning. We have ventured into learning intentions and success criteria for both individuals and groups. In this chapter, we turn our attention to the group composition. As you might predict, we don't leave this to chance any more than we leave task design or learning targets to chance. For collective student efficacy to develop and flourish, teachers must be intentional and design experiences for students. And they must take note of their impact and make adjustments when the outcomes are less than expected.

More Is Less?

In 1913, Max Ringelmann asked a series of individuals to exert their maximal force pulling a rope. The rope was attached to a fixed dynamometer, which then provided the necessary metric for estimating group performance. All one had to do was sum each group member's maximum individual reading on the dynamometer to provide a benchmark for comparing the group's ideal with their actual performance. The results were intriguing, because they revealed that the group's maximal efforts were an inverse function of group size—as the group size increased, the performance went down. This remained so as groups increased from two (93 percent of estimated maximum) to eight (49 percent of estimated maximum) members in size: there was a loss of 7 percent for each additional member. A massive law of diminishing returns (see Figure 7.1).

DIMINISHING RETURNS FOR INCREASING GROUP SIZE

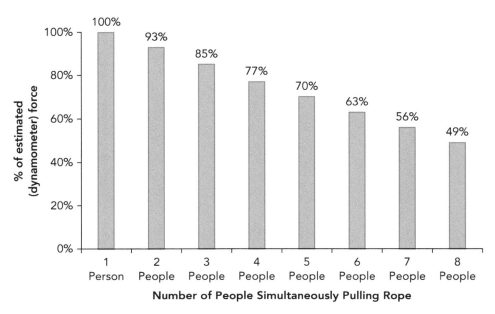

Source: Kravitz & Martin, 1986.

Figure 7.1

Ringelmann observed that there is an inverse relationship between the size of the group and the magnitude of each group members' individual contributions to the successful completion of a task. As more and more people are added to a group, the group often becomes increasingly *inefficient*, ultimately violating the notion that group effort and team participation reliably leads to increased effort on behalf of the members (Kravitz & Martin, 1986). Clearly, two to three was optimal and this is the foundation of the Ringelmann effect.

This effect of smaller groups being more successful than larger groups has been replicated many times in many scenarios. Laughlin, Hatch, Silver, and Boh (2006), for example, found performance tends to plateau when groups reach three members in size, leading the authors to conclude "3-person groups are necessary and sufficient to perform better than the best individuals on highly intellective problems" (p. 644). While there is no magic answer to group size, it does seem that as more members are added, there can be

- loss of coordination and motivation among members,

- an increased chance of a member with lower social sensitivity disrupting the group,

- a greater probability of social loafing and "free-riding," leading to group members less likely to exert maximal effort, and

- higher chances of individuals apportioning personal efforts according to their identity and dispensability within the group, as well as the difficulty, potential payoff, and expectations about achieving the group goal.

So, it is not "the more, the merrier." Recall that six to seven starlings were sufficient to maintain their amazing formations—but more led to too much mental energy to process the myriad of details needed to maintain the swarm. So, is two to seven enough?

Of course, there are some tasks that are purposefully structured to require particular numbers of members in a group. The Jigsaw method (Aronson, 1978), discussed in Chapter 3, is an example of an instructional tool teachers can use to disrupt the limits of group size because each member of the group has a different section of the text and different roles to play, and the various groupings that will occur require each student to contribute. Reciprocal teaching (Palincsar & Brown, 1984) is another instructional tool that allows teachers to use larger groups. In the typical reciprocal teaching group, four students collaborate to read a text, stopping at points to discuss. During each discussion, one student summarizes the section, another predicts what might come next, another asks questions, and another clarifies words and ideas. But reciprocal teaching is not limited to four students; two students can share a job, especially if there is a need for peer tutoring, or a student can have two roles. It's worth noting here that there are ways to increase group size, holding students accountable for their individual contributions.

Learning in Pairs

Starting with two

Is two too few? Baines et al. (2016) suggest starting collective learning by creating learning pairs. Later, once routines have been established so that pairs work productively, it is easier to start creating groups of four or snowballing pairs to work with another pair, sharing ideas. After the organization of pairs has been decided, discussions about how best to be a good learning partner can follow.

The following example is a lesson in which pairs snowballed into groups of four, sharing their ideas. The teacher's goal was for students to understand conservation of number (problem solving). Success criteria for solving problems (a transferable skill) as well as "working together" success criteria were discussed with the children. The use of an "odd one out" question is ideal for shared discussion, as students have to convince each other that their explanation is the right one.

The teacher's account describes the process and the outcome of observed collective efficacy:

MATH PROBLEM SOLVING (FOUR- TO FIVE-YEAR-OLDS): PAIRS, FOURS, THEN WHOLE CLASS

Learning intention: We are learning to find different ways of making a number (conservation) COMPENSATORY (merging all skills)

Task: Which is the odd one out?

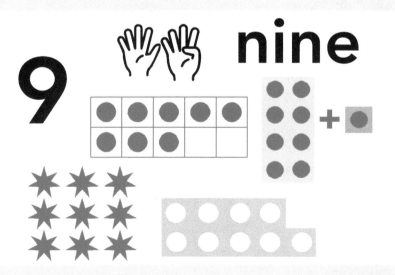

Figure 7.2

Success criteria (transferable problem solving):	Success criteria for talk partners (permanent display):
• Make a guess first • Look carefully at the information • Make sure you don't miss anything • Check your answer	• Listen to each other • Don't interrupt • Be kind • Share ideas • Help each other

Teacher's Account

"When delivering this math lesson starter, the children were asked to talk to their partner to spot an 'odd one out' mistake on the whiteboard (see Figure 7.2). It became apparent that several pairs had agreed on an incorrect answer. In other pairs, a more confident partner was persuading their partner to change their correct answer. I asked the pairs to turn to create groups of four. Each group had someone with the correct answer. The children were asked to explain to their group how they had solved the problem and to prove that they had the right answer. After a short discussion, all children were able to understand the question and prove that their group answer was correct.

"The explaining had convinced the children who had the incorrect answer but also had helped them understand what had gone wrong. There was tangible collective efficacy in the class—a passionate belief that they knew the answer, had worked it out for themselves, and could prove it!"

Emma Shiland, Ysgol Glan Gele Infant School, Abergele, Wales

The success in this lesson was that these four-year-olds were not taught about conservation first—they were shown the pictures and had to discuss which was the odd one out. Their discussions led them to clear understanding, between the whole class in the end, that the odd one out was the one that was not the number nine. They learned about conservation through this motivating task. The teacher then followed up with specific lessons where they demonstrated their new knowledge about conservation, and they co-constructed the success criteria for conservation based on their learning:

Remember:

- *The total of the group is how many items are in the group.*
- *It doesn't matter how big or small the items are.*

- *It doesn't matter whether they are completely different things as long as the total number stays the same.*

Our conclusion is to include about two to seven members in groups, pay attention to the roles for each member to ensure each is contributing, and evaluate (and have the students help in this evaluation) the success of group functioning and performance. There is no prescription to keep the groups constant over many activities. In fact, there are major advantages of having mixed ability small groups for well-designed tasks, as then you have a mix of teachers and students in the student group, and it is more likely that errors and misunderstandings can be voiced (even by those starting out more advanced). We know the power of peer tutoring for both the tutor and tutee.

WHO SITS WITH WHOM AND FOR HOW LONG?

Students often sit beside the same student for weeks on end. Roles become set (*"I help Helen"* or *"She helps me"*) and sometimes not necessarily in each child's best interests. Over two years, four hundred and twenty teachers in my "learning teams" experimented with different ways of pairing students: similar achievement levels, different achievement levels, friendship pairings, and random pairings. They also trialed students sitting with the same partner for three weeks, two weeks, and one week before changing partners. The results were overwhelmingly clear—random learning partners selected by a) named popsicle sticks (lollysticks or paddle pops) drawn out of a tin, or b) students numbered then the number pairs displayed, or c) an online randomizer with pairs instructed where to sit by the teacher, was the preference for every teacher in the teams. We determined the optimum time for changing partners at about one week for elementary students, and after every sixth lesson for secondary students. Students liked the fairness of the model, all in the same boat, and the impact on learning was powerful, as I described in earlier books (2005, 2008, 2014). The following is a brief summary of the many impact conclusions, from their introduction in 2001 to the present day:

- The system was all inclusive.

- Students encountered, over a year, a range of both cognitive and social partners to learn from and with (e.g., sometimes being the higher achiever, sometimes the lower).

- Behavior in classes improved as students developed mutual respect for each other and had no time to get into bad habits with the same student.

- Students experienced greater exposure to good examples and thinking.

- Students learned from each other.

- Success in one pair increased student confidence to be able to work effectively with anyone.

- Instant mixed ability meant students were not "labeled" so motivation increased.

- Student focus improved as questions asked of the class were no longer answered via "hands raised" focus but by random calling via the named popsicle sticks, so anyone could be called upon.

- Short discussion between pairs after a class question was asked (thirty seconds to one minute was the norm) meant they had "wait time" to articulate their thinking and decide their responses together.

- Making groups of threes can be helpful when students benefit from language support.

- Less teacher talk occurs as questions are repeatedly turned over to students.

- Students make new friends.

In short, we found that random pairs of students changing regularly resulted in high levels of collective efficacy as students together achieved success. A focus on the success criteria for being a good learning partner and the culture of mutual respect that develops sets the scene for successful groups of three, four, or more.

GROUPING FOR COMPLEX TASKS

When the task is complex and requires multiple sessions, it can be useful to intentionally create groups. Using random groups can result in two or three students who struggle with the content being placed together. Interestingly, Bennett and Cass (1988) found that heterogeneous groups were more successful when they were constructed so that the number of low-achieving students balanced the high-achieving ones within the group. This ensured that the high-achieving students did not take over the learning process and exclude the low-achieving members in the rush to complete the task. One way for teachers to group students for group tasks is by ranking the class by their relevant skill level, from the top performing student to the lowest performing student. Privately, the teacher then cuts the list at the midpoint and forms groups by selecting students from each of the lists. For example, for their collaborative learning groups in math, the teacher listed the thirty-two students in order of skill based on the most recent assessment. The list was cut in half after student sixteen. The second list was comprised of the names of students seventeen through thirty-two. Both lists are placed side by side, and the first two names from the first list are paired with the top two names on list two. Therefore, students one, two, seventeen, and eighteen were grouped together. Students three, four, nineteen, and twenty were grouped together, and so on. In this way, every group maintains heterogeneity, but the membership is not so different from one another that the group cannot produce.

Co-constructing success criteria for learning partners

Developing success criteria for "how to be an effective learning partner" with the whole class establishes agreed rules, which are best co-constructed, displayed, and referred to during lessons where needed. These success criteria are used for self and peer evaluations throughout and at the ends of lessons or before changing partners. The most popular strategy for co-constructing pairs' success criteria is to role play with a teaching assistant or another student, a paired discussion. The teaching assistant behaves perfectly: holding eye contact, not interrupting, nodding encouragingly, being polite and so on. The teacher, on the other hand, behaves dreadfully, demonstrating how not to be a good learning partner, interrupting, looking bored, and so on. While entertaining, the juxtaposition of excellence next to poor behavior is an effective mechanism for helping students identify the desired behaviors. This role play is followed by learning partners discussing together then brainstorming as a class all the appropriate success criteria. Figure 7.3 shows co-constructed success criteria created in classrooms ranging from six-year-olds to high school students across the UK and the United States. These agreements give students ownership over their collective and individual responsibility when engaged in any dialogue with another student as long as they are referred to by the teacher and continually discussed.

The agreed, co-constructed success criteria need to be constantly referenced to stop them from becoming ignored "wallpaper." They are referred to before each task and can be mentioned throughout a lesson to highlight where good practice has been witnessed. At ends of lessons, students can discuss which criteria they felt they were most successful at and which they needed to improve on. Evaluation slips can be created for students to complete and share, with some random asking for comments to be read out to the whole class. Examples of self and peer evaluation can be found on Shirley Clarke's Video Platform (www.shirleyclarke-education.org).

Sentence stems for learning partners

Using sentence stems when engaged in a discussion with another student gives a shared language for polite and reasoned talk. *The Core Collaborative Learning Network*, based in New York and San Diego, created the scaffold in Figure 7.4 for learners to lift the level of academic discourse related to the peer review process. The peer review process has

EXAMPLES OF CO-CONSTRUCTED LEARNING PARTNER SUCCESS CRITERIA

How to be a great talk partner (age six)	Our learning partner success criteria (age nine)	Ground rules for learning partners (age fifteen)
• No moaning or sulking • Sit close together and face each other • Speak clearly • Look at your partner when he or she speaks • Speak slowly	• Listen to my partner's advice and use it in my learning • Leave other learning partners alone • Take shared responsibility for our learning • Take turns and don't interrupt • Help my partner by offering suggestions • Understand that my partner might not agree with me • Share my ideas with my partner • Hearing is waiting for a gap so you can speak—listening is being able to let go of what you want to say and instead listening to what is being said	• Track the speaker • Convey your voice • Listen and take turns. Don't talk over each other • Disagree politely • Keep an open mind • Use persuasive arguments to express your opinion • Encourage each other • Share responsibility for learning • Respect each other • Develop your communication • Inspire each other • Don't give answers—guide instead

Figure 7.3

been outlined in the best-selling books, *Peer Power: Activate an Assessment Revolution* (Bloomberg et.al., 2019) and *Leading Impact Teams: Building a Culture of Efficacy* (Bloomberg and Pitchford, 2016). This scaffold is typically co-created with students with a goal of building a culture of efficacy grounded in empathy, patience, openness, active listening and relational trust.

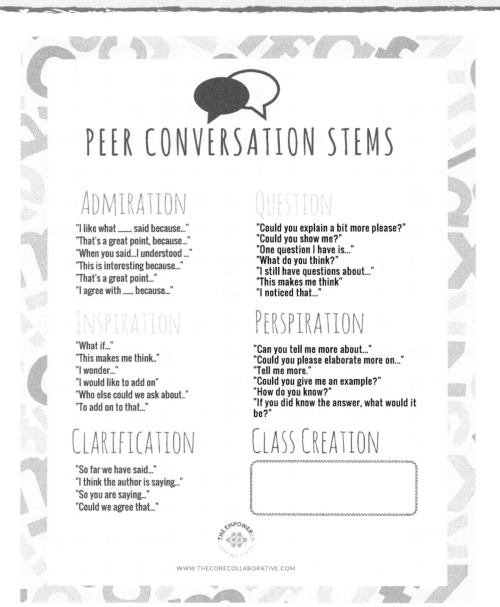

PEER CONVERSATION STEMS

ADMIRATION

"I like what ____ said because..."
"That's a great point, because..."
"When you said...I understood ..."
"This is interesting because..."
"That's a great point..."
"I agree with ____ because..."

INSPIRATION

"What if..."
"This makes me think.."
"I wonder..."
"I would like to add on"
"Who else could we ask about.."
"To add on to that..."

CLARIFICATION

"So far we have said..."
"I think the author is saying..."
"So you are saying..."
"Could we agree that..."

QUESTION

"Could you explain a bit more please?"
"Could you show me?"
"One question I have is..."
"What do you think?"
"I still have questions about..."
"This makes me think"
"I noticed that..."

PERSPIRATION

"Can you tell me more about..."
"Could you please elaborate more on..."
"Tell me more."
"Could you give me an example?"
"How do you know?"
"If you did know the answer, what would it be?"

CLASS CREATION

THE EMPOWERED

WWW.THECORECOLLABORATIVE.COM

Source: Peer Conversation Stems, https://drive.google.com/file/d/0B8kcRBjW7mrndWloTjVlbXNTbW8/view

Figure 7.4

These types of sentence stems help develop a polite, thinking, respectful culture to guide students' discussions. They are usually displayed as a poster and are used to model how discussions might evolve. Helping students know how to discuss in a sensitive way is crucial for collective efficacy to evolve where every student feels safe and listened to.

Having successful learning with a learning partner leads to greater individual self-efficacy as well, as illustrated by Rich Clayton, Derwentwater Primary School in London, England:

> *"Through weekly changing random talk partners, I have seen students improve their own self-efficacy. By having somebody that wants them to achieve and to engage with in high quality discussion, there have been examples where children make drastic improvements as they then go on to work with others. One student had produced some great writing that was obviously influenced by his learning partner. When asked about his writing, he said 'Oh, that was from when I worked with Chelsey. She helped me come up with great ideas.' His writing was significantly improved with further writing, even with different partners."*

Learning in Groups

Once successful pairs have been established, the climate is right for snowballing into groups of four or more and giving students roles appropriate for them. With the appropriate task, culture and teacher guidance, students' peer relationships are powerful, as they communicate in more child friendly language rather than "school" language and without the authority barrier of the teacher's presence.

Assigning roles

One of the most efficient ways of making sure everyone shares responsibility for involvement in the task is to assign roles. This assists in building collective efficacy when each student knows they have a role and makes it harder to social loaf. There are four major functions of groups (Nieva, et al., 1978), shown in Figure 7.5:

Muncaster and Clarke (2016) in their book *Growth Mindset Lessons* describe group roles for elementary age children in "learning groups" for tasks which require discussion and/or debate. Muncaster's experience teaching every year of the primary phase is evident in the nuanced advice for the successful development of roles and their success criteria which promote collective efficacy:

GROUP FUNCTIONS

Team **orientation** functions	How the information needed for the group to accomplish the task is generated and distributed
Team **organizational** functions	How the group can perform its tasks in a coordinated way
Team **adaption** functions	How the team members carry out the task, make mutually agreed adjustments, and complement each other
Team **motivational** functions	How the aims of the task are defined so that the team is motivated and energized to meet those aims

Adapted from: Nieva, Fleishman, & Rieck, 1978.

Figure 7.5

*"The learning groups are designed to provide a clear and coherent structure to group work which enables the children to develop a range of skills in addition to their focus activity. There are four key roles: **a manager, a recorder, a reporter, and an encourager**. Initially, it is advisable to allocate a specific role to a child and provide them with a number of opportunities to explore the same role. As the children become familiar and older, the roles can be changed regularly as this allows the children to demonstrate a range of skills.*

"Prior to using learning groups, it would be useful to give the children experience of working in this way. Initially, they could be introduced to the different roles and asked to suggest ways in which they should behave or things they should say for each role. These could then be used to create posters to remind the children how to be successful in the different roles. The children should also be given opportunities to practice the different roles. By providing the children with opportunities to discuss simple ideas, it allows them to think more about what is happening in the group and their role. This can then be further developed by activities that require the children to share differing opinions.

"When the children are working in roles, it is important that the teacher acts as a facilitator. Listen to what the children are saying—it will reveal a lot about their attitudes to learning and their individual mindsets. Try not to intervene, as allowing pupils to resolve issues within their group is an important skill for them to develop. This allows them to develop as independent learners. You could make note of the children's responses to allow you to revisit misconceptions at a later point or share ideas through a display.

> *"The use of learning groups could be developed further by children creating their own success criteria for each role, or the group's roles could be adapted or extended (e.g., the role of a questioner could be introduced. This role would require the person to ask questions to clarify meaning and develop ideas further)."*
>
> Katherine Muncaster, 2016

Different tasks and goals lend themselves to different roles. In *Powering Up Children:The Learning Power Approach to Primary Teaching*, Claxton and Carlzon (2019) describe nine roles appropriate for group discussions (Figure 7.6). If you have a group smaller than nine, you can pick which roles best suit the group's task. Instead of success criteria, each role has reflective questions to ensure the allocated student keeps focused on their responsibility.

Addressing individual needs in a group

An interesting finding from Clarke's teams' research is that random pairs that change regularly to allow for a range of cognitive and social pairings provide much support and confidence boosting for students who are lower achievers or who have speech and language difficulties. The same seems to be true for English language learners. Students on the autism spectrum tend to find the changes difficult at first, but it often becomes their "new normal." As one thirteen-year-old student on the autism spectrum said to her teacher after several weeks of weekly changing learning partners: "Talk partners have helped me come out of my shell."

Handling Negativity in a Group

Negative members can exert a disproportionately high influence on team activities and effectiveness, and their presence should be considered in team composition frameworks. Negative members can be outwardly pessimistic about the group's chances of success, put other students on the defensive, cause frustration, and encourage social loafing. If these students are not taught pro-social behaviors, this can have spillover effects and undermine group confidence.

Reluctant students often withhold their effort or involvement and thus do not fulfill their obligation to the group (and we discussed such social loafing in Chapter 2). They may express a negative mood or attitude and this can spread among other group members, introducing unacceptable behaviors such as making fun of others, bullying, acting rudely, and embarrassing others.

NINE ROLES APPROPRIATE FOR GROUP DISCUSSIONS

Role	Responsibility	Reflective questions
Note taker	Notes down key points	What are the key points? How can I summarize? What information is/isn't important?
Vocab master	Gathers interesting or new vocabulary	Which words haven't I come across before? How can I work out their meaning?
Task manager	Oversees roles within a group. Ensures everyone is clear on roles and involved in task. Might pause task to fulfill role.	Are all of my group members clear on their roles? How can I support and include all members? How can I ensure everyone has a chance to contribute?
Predictor	Imagines what might happen next	What could happen next? What makes me think that? Are there any other possibilities?
Questioner	Generates questions during task	What questions could be probing? What questions would deepen the group's understanding? What questions could I note down to research later?
Clarifier	Takes stock to ensure everyone is up to speed	Are we moving too quickly/slowly? Has everyone been clear up to now? Is there anything I can ask to help clarify? Does everyone understand what we have covered so far? How do I know?
Connector	Makes links between ideas or previous learning	Are there any links to previous learning? Are there connections to previous learning? What does this remind me of? When else have I seen/heard this?
Challenger	Challenges ideas. Plays devil's advocate.	Can we back up our ideas? Are there other possible reasons for . . . ? Does this ring true? If not, why not?
Summarizer	Sums up key points during and at end of learning	What have we discussed? What are the key points? How did we work together as a group?

Source: Claxton and Carlzon (2019).

Figure 7.6

Rather than relying on teacher intervention, we can build each student's and group's coping skills to handle these negative influences appropriately. There are four skills for handling negative influences we can teach students:

1. Recognize the right time to seek the teachers' involvement.

2. Stay calm and refrain from giving the negative students more fuel.

3. Reframe the behavior as merely a nuisance more than a substantial threat to the group's chances of success.

4. Teach replacement skills so that student's behavior is less negative.

This may lead to teaching creative problem-solving strategies to groups along with the precious knowledge and understanding; how to build trust to minimize these negative disruptions, and how to turn group conflict into conflict about the task rather than about the person.

There is no guarantee that having particularly high achieving students in a group necessarily advantages that group—there are many cases of teams with highly capable people not succeeding. The 2004 US Olympic basketball team had LeBron James, Tim Duncan, and Allen Iverson among other superstars and failed to win the gold. The team had more losses in a single year than the country's Olympic teams had suffered in all previous Olympiads combined. Yes, it probably helps to have some higher achievers, but the teacher also has to be mindful of the resources available to ensure there are performance-enhancing content and processes regardless of the attributes of group membership.

The following lesson description by a teacher reveals the real-life problems of higher achievers in a group taking over and, by comparison, the more measured approach of lower achievers in solving a problem. The lesson was an eye opener for the teacher about the need for collaboration success criteria and the importance of developing ways of dealing with conflict. The absence of interdependence success criteria gives a message to students that only the task and its learning intention and success criteria are the focus, and that nothing else matters. Aaron Hall, a teacher from Thomas Bullock Church of England Primary Academy in Norfolk, England, describes in the following vignette a series of lessons leading to a group task of building a bridge. The random grouping led to unexpected outcomes with increased self-efficacy as a lasting effect for some students, but the overall impact was the need for success criteria and discussion about what it means to be a successful member of a group.

DESIGN TECHNOLOGY (TEN- TO ELEVEN-YEAR-OLDS) WORKING IN FOURS

Learning intention: I am learning about the different types of bridges, purposes, and construction techniques (knowledge)

Learning intention: We are learning how to collaboratively determine our successes and areas for improvement

Task: Design and build a bridge using classroom material which will stand on its own. COMPENSATORY/ADDITIVE/DISJUNCTIVE (*merging all skills/many hands make light work/only needs one to get it right*)

Success criteria for applying taught design and technology knowledge (transferable skill)

Remember to:

- Review your knowledge together
- Design your product, using clear labels and measurements
- Choose appropriate materials and tools and share jobs
- Test your design and look for and discuss together successes and improvements needed
- As a group, decide how to redo or refine your design and test again

Knowledge about bridges

In your group consider:

- The different types of bridges: beam, arch, truss, cantilever suspension, and cable stay
- The reasons for the different designs of the three Forth Bridges in Scotland
- Shapes which provide strength in buildings and bridges
- Stability and fixing solutions

Bridge building

"I first focused for two weeks on the 5 different types of bridges (beam, arch, truss, cantilever suspension, and cable stay)—a knowledge focus referencing bridges such as the Forth Bridges in Scotland. I then focused on design and technology, and the skills of building using classroom materials.

"The students were assigned groups randomly and asked to design and build a bridge which had to be subjected to a number of tests to meet the specifications set by me. The goal was clear and the students were highly motivated. I followed two groups closely and recorded their collective endeavors:

GROUP A (randomly chosen, but all, randomly, low achievers)

"At the start, the group had very low expectations of their bridge being able to work. I asked them why. Student A1 said he would be ok with the woodwork as he did that at home. A3 said he had also done woodwork and enjoyed it, and A2 said he could probably make the deck. Student A4 said he would be able to paint it. Their attitude began to change as they divided up the tasks and realized they might actually be successful. Every time there was a difficulty they were observed working together to find a solution.

Group B (three very high achievers and one other)

"Although very confident initially, they struggled to work together as a group. Students B1 and B2 couldn't agree on whose design they should use (they each designed a bridge separately). B3 and B4 didn't want to take sides. After the teacher intervened by saying he would choose if they didn't, B1 said they should use B2's design. Before long, B1 and B2 began to argue, accusing each other of doing it wrong.

Group A and Group C

"As their bridge came together, these groups found it wouldn't stand without them holding it up. They would normally have become despondent, but Group A noticed Group C's bridge also wouldn't stand so suggested pulling all their features which would work into one bridge for both groups. Group C agreed and, together, they completed a bridge which would stand.

"At the end of the Project, Group A and C's bridge was highly successful. Group B's bridge did not stand up. When asked why the bridge wasn't successful, both students B1 and B2 blamed each other."

Aaron went on to note the impact on some students' future attitudes and confidence:

Pupil	Pre-project Project Attitude	Post-project Attitude
Group A1	• Reluctant to attempt any learning challenges which he felt he would not be able to achieve • When he did attempt a learning challenge, he would work slowly, often not completing enough work • If any errors were pointed out, would shut down and give up • Staff often commented that he was not interested in learning; however, I felt it was more to do with a lack of confidence in his ability	• Was much more willing to attempt learning challenges • When errors were pointed out, there was much more enthusiasm to have another go understanding that this was part of the learning process • Was more positive about the skills he had and that he could achieve tasks if he put his mind to it
Group A2	• Attendance was variable as he used to complain of being unwell • If he found the independent learning task too challenging, would often complain of being unwell • Would copy work of others	• Attendance improved • Was more willing to have a go at learning challenges; however if he found it particularly challenging could complain of being ill • An increased belief in his abilities as a learner

(Continued)

(Continued)

Pupil	Pre-project Project Attitude	Post-project Attitude
Group A3	• Lack of confidence • Would have a go at independent tasks; however, if errors were pointed out he would give up or become distracted	• Gained confidence • Much more able to deal with setbacks in his learning
Group A4	• Very slow to start any independent learning challenge • Would get upset when he couldn't complete a task • Would often refuse to do learning challenges	• This pupil continued with this attitude toward his learning
Group B1	• High achieving pupil • Often viewed by many in the class as much better than everyone else, often prompted by past teachers "praising" of his achievements • Poor communication skills and often viewed himself as an "expert" • Would often talk over other members of a group, telling them that he knew best	• Confidence was reduced after this experience, and was less likely to try to take over • Tried to work as part of a group but did tend to take over still
Group B2	• Very confident and quick to give his opinions • Struggled in groups where other members did not agree with him, often leading to him becoming frustrated and argumentative	• Changed after this experience—was more able to listen to the views of other members of a group

Aaron Hall, Thomas Bullock School, Norfolk

Figure 7.7

Aaron's class had no explicit training of interdependence skills, yet still the experience led to group success positively impacting the self-efficacy of all but one of those children observed. This increase was long term—after only one group experience. Even with talk partner and group social success criteria, vicarious experiences and social persuasion (as illustrated in the "Bridges'" account) can have a profound influence on attitudes which influence collective efficacy dispositions:

> *Most students learn to persevere with hard work because they enter a community where their peers model, support and demand it. They build grit together when they become part of a team that works hard together and makes meaningful progress.*

> (Ferlazzo, 2015 in *Developing Tenacity: Teaching Learners How to Persevere in the Face of Difficulty* by Lucas and Spencer, 2018)

Learning in pairs and then groups with appropriate task, learning intentions, success criteria, and interdependence training forms the backbone of the organizational elements of developing collective student efficacy. The acid test of collective student efficacy, of course, is in how we determine not only its existence but also its impact on student learning. The next chapter explores ways in which we can assess these factors, in order to become clearer about our beliefs and claims.

Collective efficacy leads to increased confidence in the individual as well as the group.

Experience success and your self-efficacy starts to build, encouraging you to think that you could probably achieve success again.

CHAPTER 8

ASSESSMENT OF COLLECTIVE STUDENT EFFICACY

Let us remember how we define collective student efficacy as the focus of this chapter is on how we assess collective student efficacy, not how we assess individual or group work.

- Each student needs to have confidence about their ability and disposition to successfully contribute to a task or accomplish an activity as part of a team.

- Each student needs to have skills in working for themselves and working with all in a team.

- Each student needs to have confidence or a shared belief in the team's collective capabilities to organize and execute the optimal course of action.

This chapter answers the question, "How do we know when collective student efficacy happens?" and "What does success look like?"

Revisiting Success Criteria for Collective Student Efficacy

Let's start with success criteria of successful groups that have functioned well because of their collective efficacy. The Maastricht University Guidelines (2019) recommend assessments for the individual relating to each students' skills: to acquire competences to be able to learn/

work together in a group; to work together toward the creation of group product (e.g. paper, presentation, video); and to actively evaluate the process of their group work. By the end of the groupwork module, students will be able to

- decide on appropriate role and task division which leads to effective team working;
- plan group activities accordingly;
- manage the group work within the provided time by setting deadlines and milestones; and choosing if and how to meet and share/store/collaborate on the work;
- communicate, contribute, and be receptive to ideas as a group member;
- perform constructive peer review on products or contribution of group members;
- integrate provided feedback into the final product;
- present results clearly, in the form of a presentation or poster; and
- identify areas for improvement during the process of group work.

The success of the group work means the following:

- The group enthusiastically works together, with everyone involved in some way.
- The group success is articulated by the group. Protocols of sharing, taking turns, and division of labor are evident.
- Dominance of certain students is not evident because of changing roles, although one student being a leader works as long as students appear to feel happy and valued in their given/chosen role.
- They communicate well with each other.
- They focus on goals and results.
- Everyone contributes their fair share.
- They offer each other support.
- They are organized.
- They enjoy working together.
- They articulate their enthusiasm to each other to be able to work together again.

SAMPLE SURVEY QUESTIONS FOR COLLECTIVE EFFICACY

This survey can be used to monitor whole school, whole class, paired and group collective efficacy:

1. How successful do you feel in this group?

2. Does this group help you to be successful or are you successful anyway?

3. Do you like being part of this group?

4. Does being in this group make you feel you can achieve things? How?

5. How successful do you think you all are as a group?

6. As a group, what makes you all feel confident together? Or not?

7. How successful do you think you are in the task for this group?

8. What has the teacher done to make group work successful?

9. Does success in this group make you feel more confident about success the next time? Why do you think that is?

10. How well did you do as a group at this task? How well do you think you'll do at the next task together? What makes you a successful team?

Figure 8.1

Surveys and Reflections

There are many survey questions that can provide feedback directly from students to the above questions and expectations and some rubrics which can help determine how far collective efficacy is taking place (see Figure 8.1 for a sample). These surveys can be conducted while groups are working together (and thus be formative to improve the group functioning and each student's skills in collective efficacy) or at the end (in a summative manner).

The rubric for peer assessment in Figure 8.2 was developed by the Maastricht group (van Zundert et al., 2010) and they advise, as we do, providing it to students in advance. Providing most rubrics at the time of assessment or with the results of assessment has limited impact—it is too late for students to have insight on success criteria, to undertake their work aiming as high as they can go, and to find clarity about what is in the teacher's mind when they talk about quality.

RUBRIC FOR PEER ASSESSMENT

	0-3.0	3.0-5.5	5.5-7.0	7.0-9.0	9.0-10.0
Communication	Never made clear what he/she was doing to other members of the group/supervisor	Usually did not make clear what he/she was doing to other members of the group/supervisor	Not always clear what he/she was doing to other members of the group/supervisor	Usually made clear what he/she was doing to other members of the group/supervisor	Always made clear what he/she was doing to other members of the group/supervisor
	Had no idea what had to be done and could never explain anything	Had little idea about what had to be done and could usually not explain this	Did not know exactly what to do and could not always explain what had to be done	Had a good idea of what should be done and could explain this	Had a perfect idea of what should be done and made that clear to everyone
	No participation in discussions	Hardly participated in discussions	Little participation in discussions about results and progress	Active in discussions about results and progress	Made sure there was discussion between group members about results and progress
Academic input	Was absent most of the days and spent most time outside of the group	Was not present on most days and did not work in a satisfactory/adequate manner	Was present on most days and worked in a satisfactory manner	Was present on all required days, worked well, and usually met deadlines that were set	Was present on all required days, worked well, and always met deadlines that were set
	Did not show up several times	Was late/left early several times	Was usually working, but also took too many breaks		Made extra effort (extra hours, special trips, etc.)
	Never handed in anything	Handed things in far past deadline	Handed things in late	Usually met deadlines that were set	Always met deadlines that were set

	0-3.0	3.0-5.5	5.5-7.0	7.0-9.0	9.0-10.0
	(Almost) never did what was required and showed no initiative whatsoever	Did not always do what was required and showed little to no initiative	Did what was asked from them without showing much initiative	Showed initiative and came up with some ideas to keep the project going	Showed initiative and creativity in discussions to come up with new ideas to further advance the project
	Very uninterested in the project	Not very interested in the project		Quite interested in the project	Very interested in the project
	Practical work was extremely poor quality	Practical work was usually poor quality and unreliable	Practical work was usually adequate quality	Practical work was good quality	Practical work was perfect quality
	Barely did any of the work s/he was supposed to do	Did not always do the work he/she was supposed to do	Did not do any extra work	Did extra work when asked to do so	Took initiative when extra work was required
	No initiative or help in organizing/ setting up	No initiative and little help in organizing/ setting up	Aided in organizing/ setting up experiments if asked to do so	Active in organizing/ setting up	Took initiative in organizing/ setting up
	Had no idea about the project or what had to be done on a specific day	Roughly knew what the idea of the project was; did not know what to do on a specific day	Had little knowledge of the plan on specific day	Roughly knew what had to be done per day	Had a step-by-step plan of what should be done on a specific day on paper or in his/her head
	Did not contribute to the report at all	Did not contribute to the report enough	Contributed to the report	Contributed proportionally to the report	Exceptionally strong contribution to the report

(Continued)

(Continued)

	0-3.0	3.0-5.5	5.5-7.0	7.0-9.0	9.0-10.0
Reporting	Attended meetings for only a small fraction of the others' attendance or did not attend at all	Sometimes attended meetings but was usually late or left early	Usually attended meetings but was late or left early sometimes	Always attended meetings about the report and was not late or left early	Arranged meeting to discuss about the report
	Did not write any text	Written text was of poor quality and needed a lot of editing	Written text was sufficient quality but still needed editing	Written text was good quality and needed only little editing	Written text was great quality and needed little to no revision
		Lowered the quality of the report	Did not help editing and had very little part in the overall quality of the report	Helped editing and had some part in the overall quality of the report	Had a big part in the final editing and overall quality of the report

Source: The Maastricht Group (van Zundert, Sluijsmans, & van Merrienboer, 2010).

Figure 8.2

Methods of Assessment

There are so many methods of assessment that can be used for individuals and groups, depending on whether the task is more process-oriented or product-oriented. For process assessment consider the following: log books, reflection reports, portfolios, group review meetings, observations, self- and peer-assessments, 360° feedback, contribution overviews, performance observations. For product assessment, use progress testing, portfolio surveys, self- and peer-assessments, essays, reports, knowledge and understanding tests, oral exams or presentations, posters, videos, product tests and evaluations (see Guskey & Brookhart, 2019; Heritage & Harrison, 2019).

All these methods can be used for formative and summative evaluation purposes (see Chapter 6). From a formative perspective, teachers need to seek assessment information to evaluate whether the groups are working together and progressing, to adjust what happens moment by moment and respond to learning needs. They need to engage in "on the move" assessment and feedback, observing and eavesdropping during paired and grouped discussions to ensure appropriate interventions are immediate, and where and when necessary to refocus or challenge students' ideas. Immediate feedback allows success to be highlighted and improvements suggested, although interrupting when students are in the middle of a discussion is inadvisable, as their thinking will be halted as well as their talk.

Murphy (2015) collected transcripts of student talk when working in groups undertaking activities focused on either surface, deep, or transfer lessons. What is fascinating is the high frequency of occasions when listening into the students showed that they were moving beyond the surface to deeper levels in their group, but when the teachers came to the group (by observing, listening in, or engaging) the discussions fast moved back to the surface. Teachers seem more interested in "What are you doing?" "Where are you up to?" "Any questions?" or "How can I help?" mostly leading to surface questions about facts, details, and procedures. Be wary about interrupting the flow and stopping students from trialing or experimenting with ideas. Too often they see the teacher's role as orchestrating, providing information and detail, and in charge of procedure, and this is what we want the students to take over.

More often, wait and seek the students' evaluations and assessments about their work and group progress at specific times and give students clear messages and encouragement about what makes good learning, whether alone, in pairs, or in a group. We need to evaluate the level and improvement of students' confidence and the success of the collective during the learning process.

From a summative perspective, if students know that regardless of how effective or ineffective the collaborative effort was, they will be given one single grade for the group's achievement, and they will not have the same level of motivation to exercise their interdependence skills. Nor is it to their advantage to spend time helping each other when they could be putting their efforts into their own part of the task. If roles are assigned (e.g., recorder, reporter, manager, etc.), this can counteract any demotivation, because, even with a grade of individual achievement, the role needs to be carried out according to the success criteria of that role, thus benefiting the group as a whole and adding to its success. Giving a final grade or assessment for both individual performance and being an effective group member seems the best solution.

Assigning Grades and Feedback to Individual and Group Contributions and Outcomes

We talked about the most effective forms of feedback in Chapter 3, and the reminder here is that the value of assessment is more often a function of the value of feedback to the student and to the teacher about where to go next in teaching and learning, based on quality information about where they are going and how they are going toward the success criteria.

Within the groups, students can use many forms of feedback to improve the performance of individuals and the group—such as collaborative sense-making, discussing these sense-making processes, explaining their thinking to others, adopting and working from others' ideas, recognizing and dealing with confusion, and resolving disagreements through collaborative reasoning.

A core question is whether each student should receive unique feedback and grades, whether the group only should, or whether there should be feedback and grades at both the individual and group level (and then how to do it). We advocate providing feedback and grades for both individuals and the group, but there will be many times when only one or the other is appropriate. Whatever the choice, the feedback, comments, and grades must relate to the success criteria—as this also helps build the trust in teachers' claims about what is valuable to invest in learning at the individual and group levels.

Given the nature of groups, students will inevitably make varied contributions to group performance in terms of intellect, effort, and presentation quality. So first, ensuring that the rubric for success is well understood, preferably nearer the beginning of the process, is paramount. The students should not be surprised about the grading system—whether individual, group, or both.

On some occasions, we need to be cautious not to assign marks or grades to too many individual components or outcomes. In most groups, students can split the tasks up among themselves and contribute toward different aspects of the group work. These components may not be of equivalent value, may be conducted to varying standards, may require different depths of knowledge and contribution, and may need various levels of assistance from other group members. On the other hand, a group grade can encourage social loafing, and this can lead to a lower incentive to contribute for some who realize and do not welcome that their overall grade will be dependent on the effort and achievement of others. In turn, this can lead to students believing that the grades are unfair, reduce their confidence and willingness to undertake group work, and lead to less involvement in future groups.

There are multiple ways to estimate individual and group contributions:

- Ask the students to write a short reflective report on how they have contributed to the final outcomes (process and product) of group work.

- Ask students to keep individual and/or a group reflection report or a logbook outlining the group processes, involvements, and comments on the journey to the final product.

- Use a rubric (such as Figure 8.3) for each to complete.

- For some (or all), allocate responsibility for a different task or role, and then award separate grades for individuals based upon these specific roles. It may mean you have to have success criteria established for these roles. Care is needed, as some students may feel unfairly disadvantaged by their assigned role.

- Assign a group grade and provide feedback comments. This can be a great motivator to perform as a team, and we recommend that group grades are assigned, along with individual grades.

- Assign a group grade based on an averaging or totaling of the individual grades. If this is transparent, it can lead to higher levels of students helping each other as the whole group profits when everyone succeeds.

- Award a group grade by the teacher and then have this grade moderated for each student based on the individual contribution as judged either by the supervisor or the peers. This is known as the "Knickrehm method," named for Kay Knickrehm, who argued that students can gain or lose points depending on the evaluation of other students in the group. Each

BLANK RUBRIC

Name peer:	Effort Contribution to tasks, initiative, responsibility	Team work Collaboration, communication, pleasant atmosphere	Intellectual input Creativity, input during discussions, writing for assignments	Remarks or explanation
1				
2				
3				
4				
5				
6				
7				
8				
9				
Yourself:				

Figure 8.3

student grades the others (but not themselves) and is given a set number of points to distribute to other members in confidential balloting. They can give more of their points to the group's "Most Valuable Contributors." Knickrehm recommended a 0 for contributing little or nothing, 1 for contributing some but significantly less than the student's share, 2 for a solid good job (and this should be the most common score), 3 if the individual contributed significantly more than their fair share, and 4 if the student did most of the work (and can be given to no more than one person).

- Distribute a group grade between individuals. A group grade is awarded: This grade is multiplied by the number of students in the group, and then this pool of marks is awarded to the students to distribute among themselves.

- Sanctions can be introduced to modify individual grades, such as penalizing students for inappropriate group behavior like missed attendance, social loafing, or incomplete tasks.

- Johnston and Miles (2004) devised a student contribution system and told students at the start that the final grade would be moderated by self- and peer-assessment of the contribution of each member to the group project. Each group member was scored confidentially by themselves and by the other team members on a 3 to -1 scale with the following criteria: 3 – a major contribution; 2 – some contribution; 1 – minor contribution; 0 – no contribution; and –1 – a hindrance to the group. For each group member, a ratio of their rating to the group average was calculated (contribution index) and used as a multiplier on the mark for the written report. So, if an individual contributed more than an average amount for their group, the ratio would exceed 1.0 and the mark for their written report increase. This contribution measure had little impact on the final grade but had noticeable effects on the contributions of members during the group process in positive ways. The students took the peer-assessment process seriously, clearly differentiating between group members on the contributions' questionnaires.

- Cheng and Warren (2000) used a similar method. They asked each student to estimate each individual contribution to the group and then weighted the final individual student mark as the Final Group mark * the individual students weighting factor, where the latter was = Individual Effort rating/average effort rating for the group. So, if Marco was rated 4 out of 10 and the average effort rating across all students is 6 out of 10, then the weighting is 4/6. So, the final score is the group mark = 7/10 * 4/6 = 5 (4.67 rounded up).

The following Four Key Questions to Assess Student Collaboration (see Figure 8.4) get to the heart of social learning and aim to see how far students recognize and can apply the "tremendous power of the social aspect of learning and the need and desire to enhance each other's learning through shared understanding, debate and collective action" (McDowell, 2019, p. 57).

FOUR KEY QUESTIONS TO ASSESS STUDENT COLLABORATION

Collaboration Criteria	Key Questions
Push	How can others push my thinking?
	What feedback can I seek to improve my learning?
	How can others strengthen or challenge my ideas?
	How do I push someone's thinking forward without telling them what I want them to do?
Pull	How do I support others in pulling their thinking forward?
	How do I pull someone's learning forward?
Press	How do we collectively press forward and co-construct new ideas and solutions?
	How do we celebrate and challenge our individual ideas to create a better solution together?
	How do we press upon potential misconceptions, explore paradoxes, and understand the strengths and limitations of models (such as metaphors)?
Pause	How do we pause our own ideas and listen to those from others?
	How do we pause on our first response and think deeply about supporting others?

Source: McDowell, M. (2019). *Developing expert learners: A roadmap for growing confident and competent students*. Thousand Oaks, CA: Corwin. p. 57).

Figure 8.4

Data from assessments can be used either formatively or cumulatively. When used formatively, teachers can make minute-by-minute and day-by-day decisions about the next steps needed to impact students' learning. Of course, teachers also must make judgments about the learning that has occurred over longer periods of time. The key is to think like an evaluator. What is the impact of the experiences that students have had and what do I need to do next to ensure learning? The next and final chapter summarizes the thrust of this book, and the advantages of a deliberate focus on collective student efficacy.

CHAPTER 9

THE POSSIBILITY OF COLLECTIVE STUDENT EFFICACY

We start by reiterating the three core attributes that are necessary to develop collective efficacy, or the belief that we, as a pair, group, or team, have confidence in our abilities to achieve our goals:

1. Each student needs to have *confidence about their ability and disposition* to successfully contribute to a task or accomplish an activity as part of a team (individual efficacy in contributing to the group);

2. Each student needs to have *skills in working for themselves and working with all in a team* (individual efficacy in the skills to work on a team); and

3. Each student needs to have *confidence or a shared belief in the team's collective capabilities* to organize and execute the optimal course of action (individual confidence and skills in the potency power of students working in a group).

The teacher's role is crucial in helping students to believe in their self and collective efficacy, build the individual and collective skills, ensure the learning intentions and success criteria are clear for individuals and groups, construct appropriate tasks, and be transparent about the assessment processes. As noted throughout the chapters, often it is more efficient and more transparent to students when there are specifically two success criteria, two sets of assessment—one for the individual and one for the group; and as far as feasible these are complementary.

Much research has indicated the link between teacher expectations of their students both individually and in groups and how those expectations affect the interactions and experiences of the students (e.g., Rosenthal & Jacobsen, 1968; Boser, Wilhelm & Hanna, 2014; Rubie-Davies, 2015). Low expectations, often conveyed by ability grouping, body language such as sighing, tone of voice, and excitable praise when lower achievers have success, as compared to critical feedback to higher achievers perpetuate low levels of self-efficacy. Low self-efficacy leads to underachieving, which in turn fuels low teacher expectations and low expectations from fellow students in groups, and so the downward spiral continues. This self-fulfilling prophecy can be put to better use:

> *When teachers believe students can achieve, they put forth greater effort, provide additional support, and behave in other ways that positively influence students' beliefs about themselves. Students internalize positive labels and identities and, therefore, behave in ways that increase their own chances of success.*

> —Donohoo and Katz (2019)

Gains for Students and Teachers

Paired and group work in schools are the vehicles for developing skills for collective efficacy. The extensive literature on the benefits of these strategies has demonstrated that this pairing and group work help in the following ways: learning and conceptual development; school achievement; engagement in learning; time on task, speech, and oracy development; critical, creative, and analytical thinking skills; motivation and attitudes; confidence to express and explain opinions and thoughts with peers; and relationships between peers. The four-year "SPRinG Project" on paired and group work (Baines et al., 2016) was particularly significant in highlighting the power of collective efficacy through collaboration in classrooms.

The SPRinG (Social Pedagogic Research into Group-work) project was created to address the wide gap between the potential of group work to influence learning and working relationships, and the limited use of group work in schools (Blatchford, et al., 2006). It involved following twenty-one classes of students (N=1,687 students) in a program focused on developing group skills and forty control groups.

The project had two aims: First, to work with teachers to develop strategies that would enhance the quality of group and paired work; and second, to evaluate whether these strategies would result in an improvement in pupils' attainment and learning, behavior, and attitudes to school. They applied group work across the curriculum and across the school year and worked in collaboration with the teachers. The program was based on four key principles:

1. The classroom and pupil groups need to be strategically organized and managed.
2. Group work skills need to be developed.
3. Group work activities should encourage group work.
4. Adults should adopt a range of roles that encourage student independence and interdependence rather than dominating group interactions.

The SPRinG classes, compared to the control classes, increased group and decreased individual work, which led to twice as much on-task interactions, greater levels of sustained interactions and "inferential high-level dialogue" (reasoning that goes beyond the available information), less teacher directing and more of a balance of evaluating and assessing student contributions, and greater productivity. Teaching students the skills and confidence to work in groups led to

- raising levels of attainment and deeper conceptual understanding and inferential thinking;
- student behavior improving as children took more personal responsibility;
- group work doubling sustained, active engagement in learning and more than doubling the amount of high-level, thoughtful discussion; and
- the enhancement of teachers' professional skills and confidence and the extension of their teaching repertoire.

Claxton and Carlzon (2019) suggest that teachers should be encouraged to deliberately build a culture of collaboration as their tried and tested experiences also revealed advantages for teachers and students, shown in Figure 9.1

One of the exciting outcomes of successful collaboration is not only collective efficacy but also the increased self-efficacy of the individuals in the group when they are subsequently working alone. **Collective efficacy leads to increased confidence in the individual as well as the group**.

Collective efficacy leads to increased confidence in the individual as well as the group.

A CULTURE OF COLLABORATION: ADVANTAGES FOR ALL

Advantages for Students	Advantages for Teachers
• Develops independence and interdependence	• Frees teachers up to give support where it is needed most
• Exercises social skills	• Creates bonds between students, so fewer behavioral incidents to deal with
• Improves speaking and listening skills	• Improves behavior because students feel trusted
• Fosters a supportive classroom and mutual respect	• Creates a happier, more relaxed classroom
• Strengthens self-efficacy	• Decreases stress and workloads since more responsibility is given to students
• Creates class cohesion	• Increases job satisfaction because students' growth as learners is visible
• Supports inclusion	
• Shifts the classroom from competition to cooperation	
• Creates shared outcomes and understanding	
• Enables students to see that there are usually many solutions to a problem	
• Deepens empathy and expands flexibility	
• Sparks new friendships	
• Reflects real world learning	

Source: Claxton, G., & Carlzon, B. (2019). *Powering Up Children.* Crown House Publishing, Wales.

Figure 9.1

References

Adler, M. J. (1998). *Paideia proposal*. Simon and Schuster.

Alexander, R. (2020). *A dialogic teaching companion*. Routledge.

American Psychological Association. (2020, August 26). *Resilience guide for parents and teachers*. https://www.apa.org/topics/resilience-guide-parents

Anderson, L. W., & Bloom, B. S. (2001). *A taxonomy for learning, teaching, and assessing: A revision of Bloom's taxonomy of educational objectives*. Longman.

Aronson, E. (1978). *The jigsaw classroom*. Sage.

Baines, E., Blatchford, P., & Kutnick, P. (2016). *Promoting effective group work in the primary classroom: A handbook for teachers and practitioners*. Routledge.

Bandura, A. (1977). Self-efficacy: Toward a unifying theory of behavioral change. *Psychological Review, 84*(2), 191–215.

Bandura, A. (1986). *Social foundations of thought and action*. Prentice Hall.

Bandura, A. (1989). Human agency in social cognitive theory. *American Psychologist, 44*(9), 1175–1184. https://doi.org/10.1037/0003-066X.44.9.1175

Bandura, A. (1997). *Self-efficacy: The exercise of control*. W. H. Freeman.

Bandura, A., & Walters, R. H. (1977). *Social learning theory* (Vol. 1). Prentice Hall.

Baron-Cohen, S., Wheelwright, S., Hill, J., Raste, Y., & Plumb, I. (2001). The "Reading the Mind in the Eyes" Test revised version: A study with normal adults, and adults with Asperger syndrome or high-functioning autism. *The Journal of Child Psychology and Psychiatry and Allied Disciplines, 42*(2), 241-251.

Bender, L., Walia, G., Kambhampaty, K., Nygard, K. E., & Nygard, T. E. (2012, February). Social sensitivity and classroom team projects: An empirical investigation. In *Proceedings of the 43rd ACM technical symposium on Computer Science Education* (pp. 403-408).

Bennett, N., & Cass, A. (1988). The effects of group composition on group interactive processes and pupil understanding. *British Educational Research Journal, 15*, 19-32.

Biggs, J. B. & Collis, K. F. (1982). *Evaluating the quality of learning: The SOLO taxonomy (Structure of the Observed Learning Outcome)*. Academic Press.

Billings, L., & Fitzgerald, J. (2002). Dialogic discussion and the Paideia seminar. *American Educational Research Journal, 39*(4), 907-941.

Black, P., & Wiliam, D. (1998). Assessment and classroom learning. *Assessment in Education: Principles, Policy & Practice, 5*(1), 7-74.

Blatchford, P., Baines, E., Rubie-Davies, C., Bassett, P., & Chowne, A. (2006). The effect of a new approach to group work on pupil-pupil and teacher-pupil interactions. *Journal of Educational Psychology, 98*(4), 750.

Bloom, B. S. (1956). *Taxonomy of educational objectives. Vol. 1: Cognitive domain*. McKay.

Bloomberg, P., & Pitchford, B. (2016). *Leading impact teams: Building a culture of efficacy.* Corwin

Bloomberg, P., Pitchford, B., & Vandas, K. (2019). *Peer power: Unite, learn, and prosper.* Mimi & Todd Press.

Borba, M. (2018). Nine competencies for teaching empathy. *Educational Leadership, 76*(2), 22-28.

Boser, U., Wilhelm, M., & Hanna, R. (2014). *The power of the Pygmalion Effect: Teachers' expectations strongly predict college completion.* Center for American Progress. https://files.eric.ed.gov/fulltext/ED564606.pdf

Browne, A. (2001). *Voices in the park.* DK Publishing.

Butera, F., Darnon, C., & Mugny, G. (2011). Learning from conflict. In J. Jetten and M. Hornsey. (Eds.), *Rebels in groups: Dissent, deviance, difference, and defiance* (pp. 36-53). Wiley-Blackwell.

Cheng, W., & Warren, M. (2000). Making a difference: Using peers to assess individual students' contributions to a group project. *Teaching in Higher Education, 5*(2), 243-255.

Christensen, C., Allworth, J., & Dillon, K. (2012). *How Will You Measure Your Life?* Harper Business.

Clarke, S. (2021). *Unlocking Learning Intentions and Success Criteria.* Corwin.

Claxton, G., & Carlzon, B. (2019). *Powering Up Children: The Learning Power Approach to Primary Teaching.* Crown House Publishing Ltd.

Costa, A., & Kallick, B. (2009). *Habits of mind across the curriculum: Practical and creative strategies for teachers.* ASCD.

Crary, E. (1982). *I want it.* Parenting Press, Inc.

Credé, M., Tynan, M. C., & Harms, P. D. (2017). Much ado about grit: A meta-analytic synthesis of the grit literature. *Journal of Personality and Social Psychology, 113*(3), 492.

Darnon, C., Buchs, C., & Desbar, D. (2012). The jigsaw technique and self-efficacy of vocational training students: A practice report. *European Journal of Psychology of Education, 27*(3), 439-449.

Davies, M., & Sinclair, A. (2014). Socratic questioning in the Paideia Method to encourage dialogical discussions. *Research Papers in Education, 29*(1), 20-43.

Deming, D. J. (2017). The growing importance of social skills in the labor market. *The Quarterly Journal of Economics, 132*(4), 1593-1640.

Dominguez, S., Devouche, E., Apter, G., & Gratier, M. (2016). The roots of turn-taking in the neonatal period. *Infant and Child Development, 25*(3), 240-255.

Donohoo, J., & Katz, S. (2019). *Quality Implementation: Leveraging Collective Efficacy to Make "What Works" Actually Work.* Corwin.

Dunlosky, J., & Rawson, K. A. (2012). Overconfidence produces underachievement: Inaccurate self evaluations undermine students' learning and retention. *Learning and Instruction, 22*(4), 271-280.

Eells, R. (2011). *Meta-analysis of the relationship between collective efficacy and student achievement* [Unpublished doctoral dissertation]. Loyola University of Chicago.

Ferguson, R. F., Phillips, S. F., Rowley, J. F. S., & Friedlander, J. W. (2015). *The influence of teaching: Beyond standardized test scores: Engagement, mindsets, and agency.* Harvard University. www.agi.harvard.edu/publications.php

Fisher, D., Frey, N., Amador, O., & Assof, J. (2018). *The teacher clarity playbook, grades K-12: A hands-on guide to creating learning intentions and success criteria for organized, effective instruction.* Corwin.

Fisher, D., Frey, N., & Hattie, J. (2016). *VISIBLE LEARNING® for literacy, grades K–12: Implementing the practices that work best to accelerate student learning.* Corwin.

Fisher, D., Frey, N., Lapp, D., & Johnson, K. (2000) *On-your-feet guide: Jigsaw, grades 4-12*. Corwin.

Freire, P. (1996). *Pedagogy of the oppressed* (revised). Continuum.

Gagné, R. M. (1968). Contributions of learning to human development. *Psychological Review, 75*(3), 177.

Gully, S. M., Incalaterra, K. A., Joshi, A., & Beaubien, J. M. (2002). A meta-analysis of team-efficacy, potency, and performance: Interdependence and level of analysis as moderators of observed relationships. *Journal of Applied Psychology, 87*(5), 819.

Guskey, T. R., & Brookhart, S. M. (2019). *What we know about grading: What works, what doesn't, and what's Next*. ASCD.

Guzzo, R., Yost, P., Campbell, R., & Shea, G. (1993). Potency in groups—articulating a construct. *British Journal of Social Psychology, 32*, 87-106.

Hargreaves, A. (2001). *Changing teachers, changing times: Teachers' work and culture in the postmodern age*. A&C Black.

Haroutunian-Gordon, S. (1998). A study of reflective thinking: Patterns in interpretive discussion. *Educational Theory, 48*(1), 33.

Hattie, J. A. Clinton, J. C., Nagle, B., Kelkor, V., Reid, W., Spence, K., Baker, W., & Jaeger, R. (1998). *The first year evaluation of Paideia*. Bryan Foundation and Guilford County Schools.

Hattie, J. A., & Donoghue, G. M. (2016). Learning strategies: A synthesis and conceptual model. *npj Science of Learning, 1*(1), 1-13.

Heritage, M., & Harrison, C. (2019). *The power of assessment for learning: Twenty years of research and practice in UK and US classrooms*. Corwin.

Hitlin, S., & Elder, G. H. (2007). Understanding agency: Clarifying a curiously abstract concept. *Sociological Theory, 25*(2), 170-191.

Holler, J., Casillas, M., Kendrick, K. H., & C. Levinson, S. (2016). *Turn-taking in human communicative interaction*. Frontiers Media SA.

Johnson, D. W., & Johnson, R. T. (2009). An educational psychology success story: Social interdependence theory and cooperative learning. *Educational Researcher, 38*(5), 365-379.

Johnston, L., & Miles, L. (2004). Assessing contributions to group assignments. *Assessment & Evaluation in Higher Education, 29*(6), 751-768.

Karau, S. J., & Williams, K. D. (1993). Social loafing: A meta-analytic review and theoretical integration. *Journal of Personality and Social Psychology, 65*(4), 681.

Katz-Navon, T. Y., & Erez, M. (2005). When collective-and self-efficacy affect team performance: The role of task interdependence. *Small Group Research, 36*(4), 437-465.

Kim, M., & Shin, Y. (2015). Collective efficacy as a mediator between cooperative group norms and group positive affect and team creativity. *Asia Pacific Journal of Management, 32*(3), 693-716.

Kravitz, D. A., & Martin, B. (1986). Ringelmann rediscovered: The original article. *Journal of Personality and Social Psychology, 50*(5), 936–941. https://doi.org/10.1037/0022-3514.50.5.936

Krull, K. (2003). *Harvesting hope: The story of Cesar Chavez*. Houghton Mifflin Harcourt.

Kyriacou, C., & Issitt, J. (2008). *What characterises effective teacher initiated teacher-pupil dialogue to promote conceptual understanding in mathematics lessons in England in Key Stages 2 and 3: A Systematic Review*. EPPI-Centre.

Laughlin, P. R., Hatch, E. C., Silver, J. S., & Boh, L. (2006). Groups perform better than the best individuals on letters-to-numbers problems: Effects of group size. *Journal of Personality and Social Psychology, 90*(4), 644.

Lee, C., Farh, J. L., & Chen, Z. J. (2011). Promoting group potency in project teams: The importance of group identification. *Journal of Organizational Behavior, 32*(8), 1147-1162.

Locke, E. A., & Latham, G. P. (2006). New directions in goal-setting theory. *Current Directions in Psychological Science, 15*(5), 265-268.

Louie, A. L. (1996). *Yeh-Shen: A Cinderella story from China*. Penguin.

Maclellan, E. (2014). How might teachers enable learner self-confidence? A review study. *Educational Review, 66*(1), 59-74.

Martin, R. (1992). *The rough-face girl*. Penguin.

McDowell, M. (2019). *Developing expert learners: A roadmap for growing confident and competent students*. Corwin.

Muncaster, K., & Clarke, S. (2016). *Growth mindset lessons: Every child a learner.* Rising Stars UK Limited, Hodder Education Group.

Murphy, S. K. (2015). *Student conceptions of effective classroom discourse* [Unpublished master's thesis]. University of Melbourne.

Nieva, V. F., Fleishman, E. A., & Rieck, A. (1978). Team dimensions: Their identity, their measurement, and their relationship (DTIC Research Note 85-12).

Norris, B. D. (2018). *The relationship between collective teacher efficacy and school-level reading and mathematics achievement: A meta-regression using robust variance estimation.* [Unpublished doctoral dissertation]. The University of Buffalo.

Nuthall, G. (2007). *The Hidden Lives of Learners*. NZCER Press.

Nystrand, M., & Gamoran, A. (1997). The big picture: Language and learning in hundreds of English lessons. *Opening dialogue: Understanding the dynamics of language and learning in the English classroom* (30-74). Teachers College Press.

Nystrand, M., Wu, L. L., Gamoran, A., Zeiser, S., & Long, D. A. (2003). Questions in time: Investigating the structure and dynamics of unfolding classroom discourse. *Discourse Processes, 35*(2), 135-198.

Orellana, P. (2008). *Maieutic frame presence and quantity and quality of argumentation in a Paideia Seminar* [Unpublished doctoral dissertation] University of North Carolina, Chapel Hill.

Palincsar, A. S., & Brown, A. (1984). Reciprocal teaching of comprehension-fostering and comprehension-monitoring activities. *Cognition and Instruction, 1*(2), 117-175.

Panadero, E., & Järvelä, S. (2015). Socially shared regulation of learning: A review. *European Psychologist, 20*, 190- 203.

Panitz, T. (1999). The motivational benefits of cooperative learning. *New Directions for Teaching and Learning, 78*, 59-67.

Pfost, M., Hattie, J., Dörfler, T., & Artelt, C. (2014). Individual differences in reading development: A review of 25 years of empirical research on Matthew effects in reading. *Review of Educational Research, 84*(2), 203-244.

Phan, H. P., & Ngu, B. H. (2016). Sources of self-efficacy in academic contexts: A longitudinal perspective. *School Psychology Quarterly, 31*(4), 548.

Pihlgren, A. S. (2008). *Socrates in the classroom: Rationales and effects of philosophizing with children* [Unpublished doctoral dissertation]. Pedagogiska institutionen.

Pina-Neves, S., Faria, L., & Räty, H. (2013). Students' individual and collective efficacy: Joining together two sets of beliefs for understanding academic achievement. *European Journal of Psychology of Education, 28*(2), 453-474.

Pink, D. H. (2011). *Drive: The surprising truth about what motivates us*. Penguin.

Ringelmann, M. (1913). Appareils de cultur mecanique avec treuils et cables (resultats d'essais) [Mechanical tilling equipment with winches and cables (results of tests)]. Annales de l'Institut National Agronomique, 2e serie—tome XII, 299-343.

Ris, E. W. (2015). Grit: A short history of a useful concept. *Journal of Educational Controversy, 10*(1), 3.

Roberts, T., & Billings, L. (1999). *The Paideia classroom: Teaching for understanding.* Eye on Education.

Roberts, T., & Trainor, A. (2004). Performing for yourself and others: The Paideia coached project. *Phi Delta Kappan, 85*(7), 513-519.

Robinson, V. M. (2006). Putting education back into educational leadership. *Leading and Managing, 12*(1), 62.

Robinson, V. M. J., & Lai, M. K. (2006). *Practitioners as researchers: Making it core business.* Corwin.

Rogat, T. K., & Linnenbrink-Garcia, L. (2011). Socially shared regulation in collaborative groups: An analysis of the interplay between quality of social regulation and group processes. *Cognition and Instruction, 29*(4), 375-415.

Rosenthal, R., & Jacobsen, L. (1968). *Pygmalion in the classroom: Self-fulfilling prophecies and teacher expectations.* Holt, Rhinehart, and Winston.

Rowe, L. (2019). *Exploring collective intelligence in human groups* [Unpublished doctoral dissertation]. University of Melbourne.

Rubie-Davies, C. M. (2015). *Becoming a high expectation teacher: Raising the bar.* Routledge.

Sadler, D. R. (1989). Formative assessment and the design of instructional systems. *Instructional Science, 18*(2), 119-144.

Sampson, R. J., Raudenbush, S. W., & Earls, F. (1997). Neighborhoods and violent crime: A multilevel study of collective efficacy. *Science, 277*(5328), 918-924.

Santa, C., & Havens, L. (1995). *Creating independence through student–owned strategies: Project CRISS.* Kendall-Hunt.

Shea, G. P., & Guzzo, R. A. (1987). Groups as human resources. *Research in Personnel and Human Resources Management, 5,* 323-356.

Shermer, M. (2011). *The believing brain: From ghosts and gods to politics and conspiracies—How we construct beliefs and reinforce them as truths.* Macmillan.

Siciliano, J. (1999). A template for managing teamwork in courses across the curriculum. *Journal of Education for Business, 74*(5), 261-264.

Slavin, R. E. (2010). Co-operative learning: What makes group-work work. *The Nature of Learning: Using Research to Inspire Practice,* 161-178.

Steiner, I. D. (1972). *Group process and productivity.* Academic Press.

Stirin, K., Ganzach, Y., Pazy, A., & Eden, D. (2012). The effect of perceived advantage and disadvantage on performance: The role of external efficacy. *Applied Psychology, 61*(1), 81-96.

Talsma, K., Schüz, B., Schwarzer, R., & Norris, K. (2018). I believe, therefore I achieve (and vice versa): A meta-analytic cross-lagged panel analysis of self-efficacy and academic performance. *Learning and Individual Differences, 61,* 136-150.

van Zundert, M., Sluijsmans, D., & van Merrienboer, J. (2010). Effective peer assessment processes. *Research findings and future directions, 20*(4), 270-279.

Vogel, S., & Schwabe, L. (2016). Learning and memory under stress: Implications for the classroom. *npj Science of Learning, 1*(1), 1-10.

Webb, N. L. (2002, March 28). Depth-of-knowledge levels for four content areas. Language Arts. Wisconsin Center for Educational Research. http://ossucurr .pbworks.com/w/file/fetch/49691156/Norm%20web%20dok%20by%20 subject%20area.pdf

Wilkinson, I. A., & Son, E. H. (2010). A dialogic turn in research on learning and teaching to comprehend. *Handbook of Reading Research, Volume IV*, 359.

Woolley, A. W., Aggarwal, I., & Malone, T. W. (2015). Collective intelligence and group performance. *Current Directions in Psychological Science, 24*(6), 420-424.

Young, G. F., Scardovi, L., Cavagna, A., Giardina, I., & Leonard, N. E. (2013). Starling flock networks manage uncertainty in consensus at low cost. *PLoS Computer Biology, 9*(1), e1002894.

Index

10 MINDFRAMES FOR VISIBLE LEARNING

10 MINDFRAMES FOR LEADERS

VISIBLE LEARNING FEEDBACK

DEVELOPING ASSESSMENT-CAPABLE VISIBLE LEARNERS, Grades K–12

VISIBLE LEARNING FOR LITERACY, Grades K–12

TEACHING LITERACY IN THE VISIBLE LEARNING CLASSROOM, Grades K–5, 6–12

VISIBLE LEARNING FOR MATHEMATICS, Grades K–12

TEACHING MATHEMATICS IN THE VISIBLE LEARNING CLASSROOM, Grades K–2, 3–5, 6–8, & High School

VISIBLE LEARNING FOR SCIENCE, Grades K–12

VISIBLE LEARNING FOR SOCIAL STUDIES, Grades K–12

CORWIN

A SAGE Publishing Company

CORWIN HAS ONE MISSION: to enhance education through intentional professional learning.

We build long-term relationships with our authors, educators, clients, and associations who partner with us to develop and continuously improve the best evidence-based practices that establish and support lifelong learning.